"Make America Healthy Again! Right on! In a time of too much ill-health and disunity in our country today, striving for good health really is a common denominator in America. Transcending politics, race, religion, and socioeconomics, we are UNITED in wanting better health so our nation as a whole becomes better. But finding the tool to build a healthier nation wasn't easy to find, until the dynamo Shemane Nugent stepped up. Shemane shows us how to get there . . . healthier, happier, more secure, and united. This amazing "secret" of transforming yourself in just four minutes a day sounds impossible, but oh my goodness it works! No better proof is the energetic, optimistic, productive, and knock-out beautiful author herself. So, so grateful I got my hands on her secret!"

– Governor Sarah Palin

"Want to change your life? Need some inspiration? Shemane Nugent—one of the coolest chicks on the planet—has the answer. With hard-won experience and wisdom, Shemane offers a path to better health, wealth, and happiness—in just four minutes a day. And, given that she's a Nugent, there's a hefty dose of soul-stirring rock 'n' roll in there too! Read this book NOW—and within four minutes you'll find yourself smiling—and on the way to a better you."

– Monica Crowley, PhD, *FOX News, The Washington Times*

"There are 1,440 minutes in a day, and Shemane's blueprints to a healthy mind and body require only four of them. *4 Minutes to Happy* is a must read for everyone who wants to get from where they are to where they want to be!"

– Dr. David Friedman, *syndicated TV/radio health expert, international award-winning, #1 bestselling author of* **Food Sanity**

4 Minutes to Happy

4 minutes TO Happy

Be Happier, Healthier, and Live the Life of YOUR Dreams

SHEMANE NUGENT

NEW YORK

LONDON • NASHVILLE • MELBOURNE • VANCOUVER

4 Minutes to Happy

Be Happier, Healthier, and Live the Life of Your Dreams

Published in New York, New York, by Morgan James Publishing. Morgan James is a trademark of Morgan James, LLC. www.MorganJamesPublishing.com

ISBN 9781642795899 paperback
ISBN 9781642795905 eBook
Library of Congress Control Number: 2019939827

Cover Design by:
Rachel Lopez
www.r2cdesign.com

Interior Design by:
Chris Treccani
www.3dogcreative.net

Morgan James is a proud partner of Habitat for Humanity Peninsula
and Greater Williamsburg. Partners in building since 2006.

Get involved today! Visit
MorganJamesPublishing.com/giving-back

Contents

Introduction
Start Here

God speaks to people in many ways. He can sound like a subtle voice that ignites an idea or encourages positive feelings. Or He can sound like the feeling of an unstoppable force so overwhelming that there is no other choice than to move in one direction. But I never had any of those types of communication with Him. Sure, I prayed every night before I went to sleep like the good Catholic girl I was raised to be, but even after begging for a sign about ending a relationship or taking a new job, I never heard His voice, or at least I wasn't sure I did. I've always had difficulty making decisions. Well, that's not entirely true. When picking out a pair of new shoes, if the look, the fit, and the color made me happy, I felt confident about buying a pair. Other than shoe shopping, I rarely felt the push or pull to move to Des Moines and open a yoga studio or anything else. Until one fate-filled Friday.

Around the time Jane Fonda began touting exercise videos, I started teaching group fitness classes. I had leg warmers, a thong leotard, and a wide, white pleather belt. My energy was unstoppable! I could do cancans (think Rockettes) for days. I entered an aerobics competition that took place over the course of six weeks *at a bar.* Every Thursday evening the audience's cheers determined who would move on to the next week. I outlasted dozens of other competitors (let's just skip over the fact that the judges were probably a bit sauced), and I was named Detroit's Most Physical Female!

I taught fifteen high-intensity aerobics classes every week. Then I met my husband, rocker Ted Nugent, got married, had a baby, and moved to the country. I gave up my job as the traffic reporter at a rock 'n roll radio station in Detroit and focused on helping Ted raise his two teenagers and our son while Ted toured.

My health and fitness addiction was still a great passion, so I opened an aerobics studio in our small Michigan town. One day, ten minutes into my class, it felt like an elephant was sitting on my chest. I couldn't get enough air in my lungs. I was scared. I had had a few red-flag moments prior to that incident, at times experiencing debilitating migraines and chronic fatigue. I knew something was terribly wrong, but I couldn't figure out what. My son, Rocco, was sick with constant allergies, anemia, and severe asthma. My husband was tired all the time, and neither of us could sleep. Doctors told us we were just too busy—which was true—so we ignored the blatant messages our bodies were sending and chalked it up to being overworked.

My lightbulb moment came when we traveled to London. We slept like babies—eight hours for me and ten for Ted. We felt amazing! Then, when we got home, the vicious sleep cycle started again. We became insomniacs. We developed a few other symptoms too: We both had brain fog (the inability to focus and stay alert) and short-term memory loss. Remember the old handheld telephones? Once, I put ours in the refrigerator and the milk in the cupboard. Mentally and physically I was losing the ability to function normally. We also acquired restless leg syndrome *on our whole bodies.* One night, I thought a mouse or some rodent was under the sheets. I lifted the covers to find nothing—nothing but our tired and battered legs.

I felt like I was one hundred years old. My headaches were out of control—three to five migraines every week. I was hospitalized several times a year and went to world-renowned headache specialists who gave me different medications when one didn't work. I was popping pills like M & M's. Okay, it wasn't quite that bad, because I really like M & M's, but it felt like it. I knew that covering my symptoms with drugs wouldn't solve my health issues, but no white-coated medical practitioners could give me any answers or help me. I felt like an astronaut cut off from the mothership, drifting in space. I should have been the poster child for health and fitness, but I could barely make it through the day.

Every day, Ted was struggling with energy, but his testosterone—and stubbornness—helped him push through. One morning, after another sleepless night, I took an extra-long shower and cried . . . and prayed for help.

It was finally concluded that our house, which was featured on *MTV Cribs*, was actually killing us. Although we never saw it, toxic black mold had been growing between the walls. A toxicologist determined that Ted and I had four types of mold in our bloodstream, and he diagnosed me with pre-emphysema. The moment he reached into the pocket of his white coat and took out his little prescription pad and wrote, "Get out of the house," will be forever imprinted in my memory.

Mold was a taboo topic back then, in early 2000. People thought we were bonkers. We had our house tested three times before getting a positive reading for more than a dozen types of toxic mold on the walls, in the air we breathed, on our furniture, and even within our clothing. (Be wary of the used clothing you buy at thrift stores!) One mold spore is one one-hundredth the size of a human hair, and its natural defense mechanism is to propagate a million times. It takes temperatures of more than five hundred degrees to get rid of those tiny toxins.

At that time, no one knew much about how to fix the house or how to help us, but we had to move forward and move out. Since we were scheduled to film a reality show on our property, preferably using parts of our house, we rented a camper that sat on the driveway in front of our toxic home. The show must go on, right? For kitchen scenes, we used a friend's home. Saving our lives, rather than the house and stuff we had accumulated, was most important.

The microscopic, monster molecules invaded everything in our beloved home: a beautiful, five-thousand-square-foot house that stood majestically overlooking a lake with ducks and geese, a place where we had so many memories. We left the house with only the clothes on our backs and demolished the home.

It doesn't matter if you live in Antarctica or Florida; if you have a porous substance, lack of ventilation, and water infiltration, you will have deadly toxic mold contamination within seventy-two hours. Sadly, folks, it's everywhere. Even the Bible references mold and its pernicious consequences (Leviticus 14:33). If you have constant colds or flulike symptoms and you've had a water leak, please get your home tested. It might just save your life.

While a majority of the public understands that mold contamination is a real, life-threatening scenario, there are still a few skeptics, which is why I'm telling my story. I went from being Detroit's Most Physical Female to barely being able to walk up a flight of stairs. How would I take care of my son? How would I get to his after-school activities and parent-teacher conferences? What are the long-term effects of toxic mold exposure? Would my husband be able to continue playing music and touring?

I had so many unanswered questions, but I had to focus on healing myself and my family.

Testosterone is a male hormone that builds bones and muscles. Since men have more testosterone than women do, their bodies are stronger and better protected—that figures! I was in the house more than Ted and Rocco, so, consequently, I had been hit the hardest. Rocco was able to attend school while being treated for asthma, and

Ted was still able to tour with some considerations for chemical sensitivity (see Chapter 43 on Chemical Sensitivity), but I could barely function.

Rather than go to a traditional hospital that would surely advocate for prescription drugs to cover the problem, I researched facilities that could detoxify my body. For nearly a month, I was treated at the Environmental Health Center in Dallas by Dr. William Rea, a renowned functional medicine doctor who focused on healing without drugs and using alternative remedies such as an infrared sauna that can penetrate the body on a cellular level for quicker detoxification. For nearly two hours each day, an IV filled with essential vitamins, including C and B and magnesium, flowed into my veins while I breathed pure oxygen. I was on a specific rotation diet to discover how my body reacted to different foods. I was tested for nearly every allergen—airborne and food—including camel meat, since I had been to Africa many times.

Fortunately, the human body has an amazing ability to rejuvenate. A year after we got out of the house, I started feeling better and exercising again. God was preparing something incredible for me! I started teaching fitness classes again and was hired by Zumba creator Beto Perez to develop a program called Zumba in the Circuit.

Only a few years after a fatal health scare, I was traveling all across the United States and to Sydney, London, and even Paris to train instructors and share my passion for healthy living with others! Thank you, God.

The tragedy of losing my house and my health became an amazing opportunity! Perhaps turning my mess into a message could inspire others to be healthier and happier. When you lose your health and you're lucky enough to get it back, you feel unstoppable! *Couldn't sharing this story help others?* Yes, it could! *Well, then, I must write a book,* I thought. But deciding to do something and actually doing it are two different things.

Years passed, and I hadn't written one single word. It wasn't as though I hadn't tried. I had, but I was easily distracted. I used the excuse that I was too busy to finish my book. Life gets in the way, right? So one night I prayed to God for guidance. *Maybe I shouldn't write a book. Or should I?* I truly wanted to inspire others to be healthier and happier, and with nearly four decades of experience in the fitness industry, I could teach people how to lose weight without giving up their favorite foods. (I like Fritos and cupcakes. Just saying . . .) My tragedy could motivate others to live their lives to the fullest every day! It was all in my head, but not on paper. *Why am I not motivated to write?* I fell asleep with my hands clasped in prayer.

As soon as I woke up the next morning, an amazing and undeniable feeling rocked my world like never before. God spoke to me! It was not just a whisper. It was a dynamic and powerful presence that lit my soul on fire! He told me the name of the book and all the topics I should write about. Here I was, having a conversation with God! It was as if I could see every chapter and every word in hyper-speed. It was already laid out for me. I was so excited!

Until . . . God told me I should write the book in three days. *Three days? How can anyone write a book in three days?* Then I realized that I was talking to God on Good Friday. That is one particularly miraculous event: *God spoke to me on Good Friday!*

Three days? Yes! I can do that! I announced on social media and to my husband that I'd be unavailable for seventy-two hours because I was writing a book. That way, I'd have accountability—plus, I pretty much got out of cooking and cleaning for a weekend. I locked myself in my office for twelve to fourteen hours a day, writing in four-hour blocks with short breaks to play with my dogs and get some fresh air. Honestly, three days was a breeze! The stories in this book rolled off my fingertips effortlessly. I couldn't type fast enough. Through divine intervention, I was being guided to write this book, share my healthy lifestyle tips, and be of service.

Why Have a Second Edition?

You would think that becoming a bestselling author on Amazon the day this book was first launched, November 7, 2015, would be enough. I could move on to writing the next book, which is super exciting, and I can't wait to share! But I didn't. I couldn't. Something was gnawing at my psyche. God was nudging me again. I realized I could add so much more, and I have!

What's Changed?

The layout of the book is now divided into two sections: "Mind" and "Body." The chapters related to spirituality, inspiration, motivation, and mindset fall into the "Mind" category. Chapters containing information to help you transform your body, like nutrition and exercise, are in the "Body" portion.

The journaling spaces that were at the end of each chapter in the first edition of this book now appear at the end of each section.

There's more and less. I deleted a couple of chapters that I felt weren't super significant and added a lot more information to almost every other chapter.

Why Four Minutes?

Why not five or ten? Well, first, that's the way God directed me. Second, are you ready for a dirty little secret? *Sure you are!*

Most of us are incredibly busy. We work two or even three jobs to pay our bills and provide for our families. Some of us take care of elderly or ill relatives or friends in addition to working and running households. Who isn't afflicted by stress? Every year, we swear we'll start living differently to minimize the unnecessary noise and to have simpler lives. Every New Year we say we'll rid ourselves of bad habits, but within weeks, we return to our old, unhealthy, stressful ways. So, four minutes seems doable compared to all of that. Doesn't it?

Most of us can't find the time to work out for an hour four times a week, but what if I told you that you could transform your body in just four minutes a day? The dirty little secret is . . . drumroll, please . . . if you can spend more time, do it! Not a *big* secret, I know, but it's the truth, isn't it? We will find time to do the things we really want to do, even with work and family responsibilities. Four minutes can be the catalyst to start your metamorphosis. Deep inside, a part of us wants more, dreams of more, and expects more, but sometimes it's difficult to express what's in our hearts, minds, and souls. We all have challenges. Sometimes the littlest things set us up for having a plain, old, rotten day. Traffic, poopy diapers, poop on the floor—seriously, that's what I had to deal with today. One of our dogs had diarrhea during the night. By the morning, it had dried. Yuck.

But the truly devastating situations make dried poop seem like winning the lottery: Cancer. Death. Divorce. Drug addiction. Our lives are messy, and things often don't work out the way we planned. The troubling times that challenge us—our dark nights of the soul—can instead be luminous guides that direct us through uncertainty and depression if we are open to looking at our situations differently.

I Ain't Perfect

Girl, my life is anything but perfect. In these pages, you'll read about some devastating tribulations that rocked my world and the steps I used to take back my life. And you can take back yours, too! Fifty-seven years on this planet brought me to this place. While it's not what I expected, I feel amazingly blessed. The tough stuff taught me life lessons I never would have learned unless I experienced them.

Heartaches taught me how to rise above the chaos with a smile and faith.

If I Could Give My Younger Self Advice

After losing my home, my health, and my inner peace, I am grateful for the opportunity to figure out my purpose and why I'm here. I'd never want to be my younger, mousy, people-pleasing, voiceless self. Here's what I'd tell that naive, thirty-pounds-heavier, twenty-year-old self:

1. **Don't give up on your dreams.** Sometimes you might have to put your dreams on hold. (YOU'RE GOING TO HAVE A BABY, AND YOU'LL BE EXHAUSTED!) In the pockets of your time, keep planning *big*. You'll get sidetracked, but God has some exciting things in store for you!

2. **Haters gonna hate**. Get over it. Don't waste time worrying about making everyone happy. You can't. So you might as well focus on yourself and the people who really matter to you.

3. **Be selfish.** Take care of your body, your mind, and your spirit before anything or anyone else.

4. **Keep praying, girl.** God is watching and listening. The hard times you'll endure are preparing you in ways you can't imagine. You'll be on stage in front of thousands of people, inspiring them to be happier and healthier.

Final Instructions

Like weeding a garden, you might get dirty here, digging deep down into your psyche. You'll find weeds, and you'll have to work hard to get to the root of the pain or the problem. But once you do, you will have a beautiful garden and a beautiful life! Your mind will be clear, and your path will be certain. You'll be happier!

If you've ever dreamed of doing something different or fabulous, whether traveling to an exotic location, starting a business, or getting in better shape, but you don't have a lot of time, you've come to the right place. I've felt those things, too. My journey began in 2002 when I thought I was dying.

While in the early stages of my illness, I researched the effect emotions have on the body. Decades ago, I was thin-skinned, and any and all criticism often crushed me.

Although it's not my favorite thing to experience now, I don't take it personally anymore. We know the body can absorb emotional stress, which can manifest itself in different maladies. The migraines I used to get—read that again: *used to get*—could have been exacerbated by my own toxic mindset. Some of the topics in this book deal with issues pertaining to thoughts and feelings; that's because total body health includes the effects that happiness, sadness, and grief have on our bodies.

At times, however, we have no control over what we're exposed to. The air is filled with harmful chemicals and pesticides that can cause headaches and fatigue. City traffic, exhaust fumes, heavy cleaners, and little or no fresh air can set me back for days. I get weak just thinking about it.

Can Four Minutes a Day Really Change Your Life?

God motivated me to write this book. His guidance helped me gain a higher level of health and happiness than I'd ever experienced before, and He wants the same for you. Write from your heart in the journal pages and retrain your mind to look at life's biggest challenges as gifts—even in some small way. Then your obstacles can be teachable moments.

Can four minutes a day really change your life? Yes, they can. It starts with a subtle suggestion or idea. Then maybe, just maybe, the inspiration you'll receive will help you become more creative, more productive, healthier, and happier! It could be the catalyst you need to bring major changes to your life. Hopefully, you'll want to do more than just four minutes, but you have to start somewhere.

My goal is to help you discover your own true happiness and a life that is abundant, adventurous, generous, and graceful. Start. Here. Start. Now.

Shemane

Part I
———

Healthy Mind

Chapter 1
Happiness

Happiness is not something ready-made.
It comes from your own actions.
– Dalai Lama XIV

appiness can mean something different to each of us. It can make us feel a certain way or make us smile. Happiness might mean having peace of mind, good health, or lots of money. Will a new car, handbag, or job really make us so content that we need nothing else? Is there really such a thing as happiness, or is it a fantasy in an often-brutal existence?

People in developing countries struggle to find fresh water, food, and homes, while those in developed countries worry about which iPhone or computer to purchase. Do advancements in technology make us more content or more frustrated? How many of us use smartphones to record precious moments or beautiful scenery, only to miss experiencing the event through our eyes, hearts, and souls?

Religious faith can temper the harshness of reality, so is religion a key to happiness? Is a sense of self-assurance the key? How about generosity, respect, and kindness to others? Is hope a key to happiness? Remember the first car you so desperately wanted, the one you couldn't live without? Where is it now? Are you happier because you once owned it? Does fame and wealth expedite happiness?

Numerous celebrities and affluent individuals may dispute that fact. More money and more power often mean more problems.

People often look to the golden years as the ticket to happiness, but what does retirement really mean? Loneliness? Financial hardship? Many continue to work well after the time they assumed they would.

Can a loving relationship make us happier? Yes and no. Those who have the greatest ability to bring us joy can also bring considerable pain and sadness. Have you ever been dumped? When someone you love leaves you, it's difficult to look at the positives of that relationship and consider only the good times, especially because his or her absence is painful.

We search for happiness in experiences, people, and accomplishments. Those of us who love chocolate and dream of every deliciously decadent bite understand our taste buds will be satisfied only temporarily; and the result of having our cake and eating it too is not only potential weight gain but perhaps depression and disappointment as well. So can chocolate, pizza, or whatever decadent delicacy we dream of bring true happiness?

The Dalai Lama wrote, "The purpose of life is to be happy,"[1] but is happiness a right, an obligation, or the ultimate goal in life? Is it even obtainable?

True happiness comes when we discover contentment regardless of our environment, financial status, geographical position, or state of health. Just look at the elderly in nursing homes. Why are some ninety-year-olds buoyant and upbeat despite knowing they're at the end of their lives, while others are cranky and bitter?

Having experienced times that bring us to our knees might help us appreciate the beauty and joy of little things. Can finding contentment

---

1   *Thoughts Without a Thinker: Psychotherapy from a Buddhist Perspective*, Basic Books, 1995.

in each moment—the silver lining of a cloud—be a shortcut to happiness? Our minds are incredible tools. We can think ourselves deeper into negative situations, imagining what might occur and limiting the freedom of our natural, joyful state. Or we can imagine that unlimited better times are ahead. What makes you happy?

Chapter 2
Sadness

Your pain is the breaking of the shell
that encloses your understanding.
- Kahlil Gibran

We all experience things in life that bring us to our knees. Whether it's an illness, death, divorce, loss of a job, or financial troubles, uncontrollable situations can cause us great suffering and grief. At times, we feel sad for no discernible reason. This is very similar to and often related to negative thoughts. Sadness comes from a lack of meaning and purpose, a lack of hope, fear of the future, or worrying about loved ones. It's part of the human condition that we naturally have the ability to feel blissful and melancholy and everything in between. This is a good thing.

My son, Rocco, is intelligent, sensitive, and very spiritual. He studies many spiritual practices from Christianity to Buddhism. I'll admit, I stalk him occasionally on social media to see what he's up to. One day, he posted a photo of himself crying. Tears pooled in his eyes. One slid down his cheek. It's not something a parent wants to see, especially considering that two of Rocco's closest high school friends committed suicide.

I never want to miss any warning signs. So I called him. Here's part of our conversation:

Me: Rocco, I saw the pic of you crying on IG. What's wrong? Are you okay?

Rocco: Yeah, Mom, I'm fine, *he says with a chuckle— almost as if he knew I'd call.*

Me: Should I book a flight and come visit? I can be there tonight.

Rocco: (laughing) No, that's okay. Rest assured; I'm fine. It's just that people always post pics of themselves smiling, laughing, and at their best. No one posts those real moments. Sadness is the opportunity for new understanding. It's a recognition of truth. When, where, and how did it become wrong or unacceptable in our own minds?

Me: *(This is good! I remain silent on the phone and let him continue.)*

Rocco: Think of sadness as water, and pretend our human body is the Earth. When it rains in dry places, it nourishes and feeds the land. Water is life. There is no life without it. Approximately 70 percent of this world is water. Emotion is like water; it must be allowed to flow. Often, when sadness comes up in our lives, we judge it because the world we live in, especially Western culture, has programmed us to believe that the only desirable state is euphoric happiness. This is no longer the truth. Why should an emotion be wrong? Or looked down upon? Why is it less desirable than other emotions?

Me: Brilliantly said.

Rocco: As humans, we are constantly changing: New skin. New hair. New breath. New everything. There is constant regeneration. As our physical bodies change, so do our emotional states. When we prevent the natural order of our emotional state from changing, we get in the way of the emotion trying to come through, which will only clog us up and cause emotional constipation.

Me: *(Ain't that the truth?)*

Rocco: If any emotion comes up, wanting to be expressed, the inner depths of whatever is going on inside of you reveals a truth: Emotion is just a story. It's our perspective at that specific point in time. Once it passes, our perspective changes. Our emotion changes. We have the choice in every moment of every day to accept this. Let whatever is trying to happen, happen. Get out of the way.

Me: So how do you recommend doing that?

Rocco: Yoga. Meditation. We don't have to wait for a silent place to contemplate or meditate; we can do it throughout the day. Simply bring your attention to your breath. No matter what is going on, bring your attention and awareness to each inhalation. Be your own guiding light. Be your own best friend. Take the time to be there for yourself. We are fragile creatures with strong souls. Much of our internal process has been with us since early childhood. If we were vulnerable then, we are certainly vulnerable now.

Needless to say, I didn't get on a plane that night. I am grateful and relieved that my son has such a profound perspective. Clearly, his message can help heal the world. We don't often think of healing the mind, but if you aren't truly happy, ask yourself, *do I want to be*? If the answer is yes, let go of whatever is inhibiting you, like Rocco said.

Stop letting it control you and your mind. Okay, so we're not *Bewitched*. Remember that sixties TV show? We cannot jump to a blissfully happy lifestyle with the snap of our fingers. True happiness is a discipline that takes work and courage.

Being happy is not easy. If it were, more people would be happy. But where can we start? In every moment. Right now. Every day. Again and again and again and again. We have the opportunity to choose happiness—to look on the brighter, more positive side of every situation. Since we are constantly changing, we must continue to choose to be what we want to be. If that's to be happy, then do it, be it. *Try it*. Once you really start to look at your life and realize all the areas that you have neglected, you may find negativity seeping in where it shouldn't. This is awesome! Why? Because now you know. Now you see what's happening to you. Let go of the conversations about the past or the future. *Be here right now*. If you're sad, allow yourself to wade in those waters for just a bit. Then once you've had enough emotional torment—breaking down and sobbing— there's work to do. C'mon, let's do this together!

Like leaving your home vacant for months and allowing cobwebs to form, you may have let a network of problems without solutions take over, tangling up your mind. Now you've come home to see the mess.

Time to clean. Or you can just keep going on about your life as if nothing is wrong and breathe in that dust every day. It's your choice.

Build the life you want starting now. Your life is the refuge from the weather of time. But there's a hurricane outside, and the wind is a blowin'. So, let it blow. Buckle up, buttercup. Stay warm. Find friends. Relationships act as a wonderful insulation from harsh elements, like critics and bad times. Find people who help you see you aren't crazy for all those thoughts in your head. Just as importantly, look deeply at everything in your life and why you're in a particular situation. What role did you play in getting there? And, friend, you did play a role. Our days are constantly filled with choices and opportunities.

In my darkest nights, thinking about how bad things were was never helpful. While in the eye of the storm, the best path for me was to take action—after I'd had a pity party, of course. A voice inside us all makes us think it's the end of our world. The party's over. Don't listen to that voice, my friend. We can't always change things that make us sad or mad, but we can learn from them. Those people and situations that make us uncomfortable or feel depleted are actually doing us a favor. They teach us what we don't want. Sad is a great place to start.

We must accept that sadness is a part of living, but that doesn't make it easy. When my husband told me that he had had an affair and a child with another woman just five years after we were married, the news broke my heart. It devastated me. My hopelessness and anguish turned into depression and even thoughts of suicide. For several months, I found it difficult to function normally. Honestly, it was more like years.

One day, I glimpsed myself in a mirror and didn't recognize the person I had become. My smile and happy demeanor had turned sour. My brows were constantly furrowed, and I looked ten years older. At that moment, I realized I needed to snap out of this suffering state or it would ultimately affect my health—and give me those horrible frown lines.

The Buddhist faith tells us that misery and a lack of happiness are natural states and that change is the only constant. Although change is often viewed as a negative, sadness can also be an opportunity in disguise. We think we have our lives planned, but then something dreadful happens that throws us off-kilter. Perhaps there is a greater reason for us to endure an occasional roller-coaster ride; it can help us determine exactly what we want and don't want. And if you've ever been on a roller coaster, you know there's no getting off in the middle. You better just hang on!

As I look back at some of the things that were devastating or disappointing in my life, I realize that by experiencing those turbulent times, I came to understand myself more. I became stronger. But how do you get through the eye of the storm alive? It's a process, girlfriend. Be kind to yourself during those times. Hopefully you're a faster learner than I was.

Chapter 3
Purpose

Achievement of your happiness is the only moral purpose of your life, and that happiness, not pain or mindless self-indulgence, is the proof of your moral integrity, since it is the proof and the result of your loyalty to the achievement of your values.

– Ayn Rand

D o you ever ask, why am I here? The questions and statements posed throughout this book will help you ascertain your purpose in life. By describing joy, health, prosperity, and happiness in my writing, I hope your path will become more obvious. When you know your purpose, it's easier not to get sidetracked with people, places, or things that steal your thunder. But how do you know your purpose?

If you were planning a long and fairly dangerous hike up a mountain, you would carefully plan your route and pack a first aid kit, extra socks, food, water, and a cell phone in the event that you were injured or needed help. This book will help you take a good look at the trail that led you to where you are now and to course correct, if necessary. Like climbing a mountain, there will be challenges. You may run out of food, water, or soul-fulfilling nourishment, but reaching the top of that mountain—let's call it the Happiness Mountain—far outweighs potential dangers.

Because if you're not happy right now, do you really want to continue on the same rocky path?

You've picked up this book for a reason. Perhaps you want to find peace of mind or contentment. We all experience trials and tribulations, and your life hasn't always been easy, happy, or fun. When climbing a mountain, you encounter hard angles and passes you don't think you can maneuver, but you do. Somehow, you make it past one and then another. *You're evolving.* You have grown as a person. You know what you want and what you don't want, or perhaps you're just starting to figure it out.

Things don't always happen exactly as planned, and perhaps that's because you're not ready for success or happiness. There are lessons you still need to learn, a bigger mountain for you to climb. Those lessons don't come easily, but you'll discover more prosperity, peace of mind, and bliss through patience and practice while breathing through the challenging terrain. You find your purpose when you find the thing that makes your heart sing. For each one of us, that's something different.

My daughter-in-law and her cousin invited me to climb Camelback Mountain in Arizona. During the ascent that would bring me over a mile into the sky, I didn't think I could take another step, but then I did. My legs were quivering, my feet hurt, I was tired and thirsty, but I kept moving forward. It didn't help that the girls were half my age. Of course, they weren't panting as heavily as I was. Of course, they had more energy. I placed one foot on solid ground and then the other. At one stop, I looked back and saw the vast landscape and city below. I was halfway up the mountain! Almost there! About forty-five minutes later, I made it to the top. The breathtaking city views were spectacular, and that journey is something I'll remember forever. If I had chosen to stay in bed that morning, I never would have had that triumphant experience. Sometimes we have to step out of our comfort zone to truly experience the joyful moments that set our souls on fire and help us understand who we are and why we're here.

What if we look at all our obstacles as opportunities, as mountains to climb? Sometimes, the going gets tough. We have a hard time moving forward and taking the next step. Check in with yourself on occasion. Load yourself up on the praise, in case no one else does and in case the negativity seeps in. *You're doing great! You're almost there!* Then one day you might just find yourself at the summit—your purpose in life.

But you'll never know what that is unless you keep trying every day.

Chapter 4
Values

love this quote from Mark Twain. People are surprised when others do the right thing. Consider the following story.

The evening news programs typically end with a "fluff" story. After all the political debates, hurricanes, and murders, it's nice to close with something positive. Last night I watched a story about a group of middle school boys who saved a woman from committing suicide. They saw her holding on to the side of a bridge, hanging in the air. They could have chosen to watch her fall to her death, or worse, videotaped the tragedy with their cell phones. Instead, they called their coach, who was a mentor to them.

I got the feeling that the boys didn't have many other positive role models in their lives. The coach told them to call 9-1-1 immediately, then run over to where the woman was, about fifty yards away, and try to talk her out of ending her life. "Tell her that her life is worthwhile," the coach instructed. I can imagine the sense of urgency these boys felt.

It was a life and death situation that, because of them, didn't end in a catastrophe.

People are grateful when you do the right thing, especially when you really don't have to. You'd think that a group of seventh and eighth grade boys would have been mischievous, taunted the woman, or stood by doing nothing. What's surprising is that they acted heroically, even at such young ages.

What causes people to do the right thing when no one is looking? Do you let the cashier know she didn't charge you for an item? Do you chase down a napkin that flew out of your car when you opened the door? We all make mistakes. Absolutely none of us is perfect. But how do you treat others—and yourself—when there are missteps? Do you surround yourself with people who share your values and do the right thing most often? Describing these ideals may disclose pertinent information about what you believe to be acceptable and desirable for the life of your dreams.

Chapter 5

Love

*The hunger for love is much more difficult to remove
than the hunger for bread.*

– Mother Teresa

Sometimes we let days, months, or even years pass without telling people we're close to that we love them. Whether they're grandparents or old friends, don't ever miss an opportunity to tell others how much they mean to you. You've heard the stories before—someone dies in a tragic accident and a surviving relative or friend admits they hadn't expressed their love.

We all need physical affection, too. Babies born without the benefit of loving touch will not thrive. In fact, they will die. In 1944 the US government commissioned a study to determine the effect restricting physical touch would have on babies. Within a few months, the study was halted because half of the infants died. I can't imagine watching tiny babies lose the interest and will to live. A loving gesture and gentle touch will uplift people of all ages, especially in times of distress.

I once had the honor of being a "hugger" for troops returning from active duty. Some of the brave men and women taking their first steps on US soil were en route to their home states and did not have anyone to greet them. Hundreds of family members and friends filled the stands of an outdoor football field. A marching band played music, and children dressed in their Sunday best held signs that read, "Welcome Home, Daddy." It was a festive affair. And when four buses loaded with soldiers pulled up on the opposite side of the field, the excitement and anticipation escalated.

My task was to look for the men and women who got off the bus and walked alone with no family or friends to greet them. Even in the chaos and commotion—children running into the arms of their parents, group hugs, and marriage proposals, too—the loners were easy to find. They were without smiles. But after something so simple as a hug and words of thanks for their service, their demeanor changed completely. They were happy that someone had acknowledged and appreciated them.

Take four minutes to call or write someone you love and say how thankful and blessed you are to have him or her in your life.

Chapter 6
Balance

*You can have it all, but you can't have it
all at the same time.*

– Madeleine Albright, *former US Secretary of State*

Having balance is very personal. You can have a great job, wealth, a wonderful relationship, exciting travel, a terrific family, and a social life with friends you adore, but you may not have all those things at the same time. Something has to give. Putting the most important things first is my main goal. To write this book, I carved out time that wouldn't conflict with my other responsibilities of producing and cohosting a TV show, teaching fitness classes, doing charity work, and engaging in family time—which meant time with my dogs, too!

I found a weekend that wasn't booked with obligations and stayed in my office for up to fourteen hours each day. It was an incredible amount of work, but I accomplished something important, something that was on my bucket list.

During those days, however, I didn't make dinner, didn't call my friends, or check social media or emails, and I gave up my workouts and leisure time. Those were the sacrifices I chose to make. The kids were grown and out of the house, so my time commitment to family differed from when I was a stay-at-home mom.

Working moms and dads have to make the most sacrifices. How do you choose between working late on a project versus watching your child's basketball game? There's always a sacrifice when it comes to parenting. If you're a single parent doing most of the housework, working a full-time job, and raising school-age children, you're probably working around the clock. Aren't you? You're the reason I wrote this book. You have to put yourself first, even for as little as four minutes a day.

When Ted and I got married, I quit my job as the traffic reporter at a Detroit radio station and moved into Ted's country home, away from my family and friends.

Most of the year, Ted toured and I stayed home raising Rocco and my stepchildren, Sasha and Toby. At times, I missed my job and being productive and having an occasional girls' night out. Based on my priorities at that time, I chose to sacrifice a career to be a stay-at-home parent. I don't regret that choice. Kids grow up and leave home. And for those of us who've given up our careers to raise and nurture our children, we may have some frustration or regret that we didn't use our degrees or gifts to continue working. Creating a master plan to accommodate family, fitness, work, relaxation, kids' school activities, and other obligations is essential to having balance.

We can have it all, perhaps just not simultaneously.

Now that I am an empty nester, I get to put myself first—just as flight attendants encourage you to do when they ask you to put your oxygen mask on before assisting children. Putting yourself first feels wonderful and strange at the same time. Every day I get better at saying no to activities that don't serve me.

Chapter 7
Failure

*We seem to gain wisdom more readily through our
failures than through our successes. We always think of
failure as the antithesis of success, but it isn't. Success often
lies just the other side of failure.*

– Leo Buscaglia

Many celebrities, Fortune 500 executives, and insanely wealthy people failed before they found success. Sara Blakely, founder of Spanx, is one example. Now a billionaire, Sara failed her law school entrance exam and was turned down when initially pitching her idea for women's hosiery. She didn't give up. Jim Carey was once homeless. Bill Gates's first business failed. Basketball great Michael Jordan was cut from his high school basketball team. During his career, he missed dozens of game-winning shots and over nine thousand attempts at baskets. His success story is even better because he failed but kept trying until he became the best.

We've all fallen short of goals and dreams. Leaders are the people who fall down but get back up every time. Having an idea and acting on it requires great risk, but you'll never experience considerable rewards if you don't take chances. The world needs more inspirational people to move us into consciousness and show us that through defeat we can rise to the top. Our missteps teach us what we want, don't want, and how to become more efficient.

Embrace the inner wisdom that encourages you to step outside your comfortable world and try a new activity or workout. If there's an idea brewing in your mind for weeks, months, or even years, perhaps that's your soul searching for something. Make a list of a few crazy-but-achievable goals. If you fail, that's just God guiding you into something better. Get back up and try again, girlfriend. You got this!

Chapter 8
Busyness

*If you spend too much time thinking about a thing,
you'll never get it done.*

- Bruce Lee

When I owned and operated an aerobics studio, eight fitness instructors taught classes along with me. We offered thirty classes a week and had hundreds of members. One instructor had a pretty good following, so I wanted to make sure she was happy. The feeling wasn't mutual. She went out of her way to ignore me, although I was the one signing her paycheck. One day Janice (let's call her that) walked in early before her class. I was the only other person in the studio and said hello with a bright, cheery smile. Eyes fixed forward, she didn't even acknowledge my presence. "Janice, is there something I've done to upset you?" Finally, she turned and with a cold, stern look said, "No, I just don't have any patience for people who run around and look like they're busy but accomplish nothing."

Wow. That was bold. I should have said something just as catty right back to her, but I froze. I've learned a lot since then and won't allow someone to talk to me that way. But I wondered, do others think I'm too wrapped up in the busyness of business? Are you?

Do you neglect necessary tasks like paying bills or returning phone calls because a) there are too many, and it's overwhelming, b) you may as well wait till you have more time to get it all done at once, c) the laundry is piling up, the dog's toenails need to be trimmed, and the cat got out of the bag?! Basically, excuses.

The definition of crazy is doing the same thing repeatedly but expecting a different result. If you don't seem to have enough time to do the things you need to do, apply a different strategy. We're inundated with busyness: cooking, cleaning, work, parent-teacher conferences, and those occasional, time-consuming activities we'd prefer not to do (cleaning toilets, giving pets a bath). How much time each day do you do unnecessary activities such as checking social media, posting photos on Instagram, or tweeting about a new movie? Multiply that times seven. Are you thinking what I'm thinking? A setting on most cell phones will alert you to the amount of time you've been using social media. Mine is set for an hour every day. Five minutes here, twenty minutes there—it adds up, girlfriend. We can accomplish more by doing less on social media. I know it's tempting to see those cute puppy pics. I could watch the funny pet videos for hours, but I limit myself to a few minutes at a time.

What would you do with an extra hour or two each week? By eliminating a few superfluous activities, you can reclaim a substantial amount of time to take care of the business you've been avoiding. How 'bout we start now? Spend four minutes today takin' care of business!

Chapter 9
Money

*Choose a job you love, and you will never have to work
a day in your life.*
– Confucius

D oes going to work make you anxious, stressful, or tense? Does
your job give you tension headaches and stomachaches? How
about the traffic and the commute? Frustrating, huh? Those
are wake-up calls, and over time, you could end up with high blood
pressure, high cholesterol, or even cancer. If you don't love your job,
change it or find a way to make it more enjoyable, but for goodness sake,
stop complaining about it. We have so many amazing opportunities
to become gainfully employed, even part time from home. So, if the
nature of what you do to pay the light bill negatively impacts your
physical and emotional well-being, consider other options.

Have you ever felt that your life's work should be something other
than what you do now? Do you ever imagine yourself in a different
career, making more money and feeling happier? Many of us dream
about having different, more exciting careers, but what if we could
actually make those dreams come true?

Are the wheels spinning in your mind? If so, take a moment to
think about what you would do for a career if you could do anything.
What were the things you liked to do as a teenager? Okay, I was a
cheerleader in high school, and there are no jobs for middle-aged

cheerleaders. Wait! As I write this, a new movie just came out about older women trying out for a cheer squad called *Poms,* starring Diane Keaton. You see? There's always a chance your dream job is available!

Seriously, though, what's stopping you from changing jobs or careers? If you're stuck in a meaningless position for the pay or insurance, think about something positive in your job and how it's benefiting others. Let's say you roll toilet paper for eight hours a day (work with me here). Obviously, we all need toilet paper. Have you ever been without it when you needed it? Or have you only had one square for an eight-square job? Maybe that toilet-paper-roller job is paying big bucks and has amazing insurance and ridiculous benefits. Maybe they offer massage Mondays on the rolling floor, and everyone gets a free neck rub. Admit it. You're starting to like this job already! You see what I'm doing, right? It's about the mindset. And if you cannot find anything good about what you do to earn a paycheck, it's time to look for options.

The American dream is not just about freedom; it's also about prosperity. And who hasn't spent time trying to figure out how to make more money? Admit it. You're pondering making a lot of money doing something you love, right? Wouldn't it be great to use one of your many God-given gifts to change the world? All it takes is one creative concept. Maybe you've tried, had multiple interviews, and weren't hired. Well, there's this thing called the internet.

The internet has amazing resources to help you create a business you love. Websites can help you design, create, or patent a product. Free tutorials and online programs can teach you how to give piano lessons online, write a bestselling novel in your spare time, or train your dog to do tricks. The resources are endless! Spend four minutes exploring options on how to make more money doing something you love.

Chapter 10
Effort

Doing your best is more important than being the best.
- Zig Ziglar

No matter what your job is or how menial you think it is, it's obviously important to the person who pays your salary, so show up with a good mind and spirit. If you have a job, consider yourself fortunate. Don't cut corners. Instead, go beyond your job description. Smile. Go the extra mile and be helpful to everyone you encounter.

As a teenager, my husband worked as a gas station attendant. He cleaned windshields and pumped gas. Once, when using the station's restroom, he noticed how dirty it was. So he did something most people would consider "not their job" and cleaned the toilet and the entire restroom thoroughly. When the station manager saw the result, he called all the employees into his office and demanded to know who had cleaned the restroom. Ted's coworkers had no idea what he had done. Finally, Ted admitted he was the culprit, and although he had just started working at the station, his efforts were rewarded with an immediate raise. Do your job well and with a gloriously happy attitude. People will notice!

Chapter 11
Opinions

Don't let the noise of other's opinions
drown out your own inner voice.
– Steve Jobs

f you're not happy with the way things are, then change 'em! At least make an effort to contact a politician or someone in authority about something you disagree with or, even better, compliment them.

Many of us watch the news in frustration, but few of us voice our opinions and let our feelings be known. People in authority, especially our elected officials, are interested in our viewpoints, or at least they should be.

Tell the barista at a coffee shop if your drink isn't prepared the way you requested. We pay a lot of money for a fancy cup of coffee these days. You might feel uncomfortable at first, but you should get exactly what you want. From a business owner's perspective, I'm sure they would want to know if their staff cut corners in any way. If there's a slippery floor that could potentially be dangerous for an elderly person, don't you think the owner would rather take care of the problem before something disastrous happens? We don't want to come across as divas, so adjust your tone of voice and ask nicely. You might be surprised at the result.

Chapter 12
Environment

Love is in the air, but the air is highly polluted.

- Anonymous

You don't realize how much litter can ruin the look of a community until you drive through areas with well-kept lawns, watered and healthy colorful flowers, and no litter—no empty water bottles, pop cans, or trash clogging the road drains, no scraps of paper blowing in the wind. When people tend to their homes and communities and take pride in their environment, it's pleasant to see. And an environment devoid of excess debris can improve our overall health, too. Ever visit New York City on a hot summer day? The stench can assault your senses. Rodents, stray cats, and dogs feed off food scraps left in paper and plastic wrapping in the streets. Bacteria from the rotten food is spread throughout the neighborhoods and into homes, where cockroaches squeeze in between walls and floors.

When I visited Tokyo, I noticed very few receptacles for waste. It's hard to find them on the street, and when you do, they are usually very small and typically have lots of recycling options for sorting trash. Kamikatsu, known for being a town with net zero waste, has thirty-four types of bins for separating paper, plastic, aluminum, electronics, glass, food, Styrofoam, etc. Small metals like lipstick tubes go in one container, while the unused lipstick goes in another. Everyone has their own hand towels to use after washing. Think about how much time, energy, and money we would save if we each did that!

Another reason the streets in Tokyo are nearly pristine: The Japanese culture takes eating seriously. Japanese people don't use take-out as much as most Americans. Meals are enjoyed while sitting down, relaxing, and eating slowly.

Where does the trash go? It goes between Japan and the West Coast of the United States, making up a floating island of toxic plastic waste that scientists call the Great Pacific Garbage Patch. There, marine life is threatened by tiny pieces of plastic they ingest. It's so large that it would take decades to clean up, and that's without adding more debris. It's disgusting, and it makes me want to up my recycling game.

Another type of environmental pollution, or energy vampire, swirls around you, and you may not even know it. Electromagnetic frequency (EMF) is an invisible energy system that can bust through concrete and steel. EMFs are emitted from cell phones, alarm systems, televisions, microwaves, blenders, alarm clocks, and, yes, our beloved internet. Even at low levels, EMFs can cause headaches, joint pain, memory loss, insomnia, seizures, low libido, and cancer.[2]

A holistic approach to minimizing harmful radiation can be simple. Appliances, cell phones, and computers, even in the "off" position but plugged in, can be energy vampires. Unplugging lamps, coffeemakers, and televisions when you're not using them will save you hundreds of dollars a year and reduce EMFs. As we will discuss in the "Sleep" chapter, keep electronics away from your bed. Placing crystals like black tourmaline and quartz around your laptop can also help minimize EMF.

Do your part to safeguard the environment by cutting back on unnecessary energy consumption and consuming less. Recycle and

---

2   https://www.who.int/peh-emf/about/ WhatisEMF/en/index1.html)

reuse whatever you can. Heed these tips for turning your trash into treasures:

- Use glass soda bottles for wildflower displays.
- Turn unused scarves into bows on gifts.
- Take old crates and make a table.
- Reuse gift boxes.
- Take your own glass containers to use for carry-outs.
- Get a water purification system.

It's our duty to take care of the environment in which we live, work, and play. When you see something, do something. Go out of your way to pick up someone else's litter to safeguard your community. It's shocking to think that getting rid of our waste is a big problem, but it is. Let's take care of our environment.

Chapter 13
Plan

By failing to prepare, you are preparing to fail.
– Benjamin Franklin

When disaster strikes, whether due to Mother Nature or a manmade attack, you'll look for a doomsday prepper near you. I'm not talking about building an ark and planning for a Noah-type flood, although there's nothing wrong with that; I'm just hinting about being prepared for minor or major catastrophes. We have fire extinguishers and first aid kits in our homes, right? Natural disasters, such as hurricanes, tornados, and earthquakes, can leave you and your family without electricity, food, water, shelter, or access to money and medication for days, weeks, even months.

It's important to have a plan. Where would you go? What would you do if you had to start over because of a flood, fire, or something worse? Experts suggest planning for three months without food, electricity, or water. Along with the basics of canned and dried foods for our home, we have backpacks with first aid kits, flares, ropes, food, water, and other essentials in our vehicles, too.

Consider archery. When the Y2K fears came around, family members and friends asked if they could stay with us. They knew that as hunters we live off the land. Our protein sustenance comes mostly from grass-fed venison. Thankfully those conspiracies about losing power in the year 2000 fizzled and grocery stores were stocked with plenty of food. But if that were to happen, we wouldn't miss a meal.

The new house we are building will have solar backup so that we can continue to enjoy conveniences like light and refrigeration if a catastrophe were to occur.

Don't forget about your pets. Have extra food and medicine stored for them, too. Even dog food has an expiration date, so write it with a bold marker on the side of the product. When you check supplies, you can easily see when you need to swap out older food.

Things to have on hand:

- minimum three-week supply of high-energy food like peanut butter, nuts, canned fish, and meat
- one gallon of water per person per day
- medication
- matches, candles, flashlights
- first aid kit
- battery-operated radio
- flares, ropes, plastic bags
- emergency exit route from your city
- phone numbers of family members

Let's hope we never need these supplies.

Chapter 14
Read

Education is the most powerful weapon
you can use to change the world.
– Nelson Mandela

Educated people tend to be healthier, happier, make more money, and live longer. They have better job stability and health benefits. With so much information available at our fingertips on the internet, there's no reason we can't learn something new, read a newspaper, or research ideas online. Reading lowers blood pressure and helps fight depression by keeping our minds active. People who have higher levels of education typically take better care of themselves and are more involved in improving society.

My sleep aid is reading. I like to get lost in another world that relieves my mind from the busyness of the day. When I travel or have too many projects, I can't seem to stop my mind from spinning. After a relaxing bath, I snuggle up on the bed with my dogs and a good book. Then, the trials of the day seem to fade. Sometimes I can only read a few pages before my eyes start closing.

Reading relieves boredom, especially in older adults. Quite a few online courses don't require previous experience or even education, so take advantage. You can even learn for free!

Here are some tips on seeking higher education:

- Pick a topic that fascinates you.

- Search online for learning programs.
- Go to a bookstore and browse trade magazines or books.
- Join a book club or another group that will make you accountable to read more.

Chapter 15
Language

To have another language is to possess a second soul.
- Charlemagne

The most important reason to learn another language: It can help you communicate with people from (or in) different countries. If you've always wanted to travel to France, learning to speak French would be beneficial.

Sometimes, the task is so daunting that we don't even know where to start, so we don't start at all. Many incredible language-learning programs are available on the internet for free. Start small and cheap. If you really enjoy the language and the program, take the next step: Purchase or download an interactive program. You can even get coaching online.

Learning another language stimulates your brain cells and helps them grow. It can ward off dementia and even depression. In addition, you'll learn about a different culture and have more compassion for the people who live there.

The top ten most spoken languages are:

5. Mandarin Chinese (1.1 billion speakers)
6. English (983 million speakers)
7. Hindustani (544 million speakers)
8. Spanish (527 million speakers)
9. Arabic (422 million speakers)

10. Malay (281 million speakers)
11. Russian (267 million speakers)
12. Bengali (261 million speakers)[3]

Chapter 16
Travel

It is good to have an end to journey toward, but it is the journey that matters, in the end.
– Ernest Hemingway

Traveling offers us many opportunities to cultivate awareness of other cultures and expand our understanding of what it's like to live in another country. We also learn to appreciate what we have back home. Looking at the architecture, tasting the food, and watching the way people interact in another country can teach us more than we could learn from any book. We can discover more about our inner connections to humanity in areas of dire poverty and learn that politics just don't matter when there's nothing to eat.

Imagine opening a beautifully wrapped gift. You shiver with anticipation. The box feels light, but maybe it's a ticket to that place you always wanted to visit—let's say Paris. You pull back the tissue paper to see a postcard of the Eiffel Tower. The gift-giver says, "I know you wanted to go to Paris, but here's a great picture instead! Feels just like we're there, right?" Wrong.

Waking up each morning to the sights and sounds of a different country envelops your senses in a way that no picture or video can. I've traveled to Africa many times and am grateful for having witnessed remarkable wildlife, rolling topography, and even impoverished conditions. To see a herd of zebra in their natural habitat or giraffes nibbling on treetops nearby is an extraordinary sight that no brochure can adequately describe. Your perception changes about a culture when you experience it firsthand. Getting out of your comfort zone and your zip code can offer you many amazing health benefits as well. Traveling can help you live longer, decrease stress, and minimize your risk of heart attacks.[4]

Guys, listen up! Your mortality rate increases by 20 percent if you don't take vacations. So many of us feel guilty for taking time to explore other regions, but at times, even a short trip might be just what the doctor ordered.

4   https://www.latimes.com/travel/la-trw-vacation16jul16-story.html

Chapter 17
Music

Music is what feelings sound like.

- Unknown

magine that you're in a bad mood. Not likely to happen, right? Ha! We've all been there. Maybe we're missing someone, traffic was horrible, the dog pooped in the house, and the baby's diaper didn't exactly catch everything. *Been there. Done that.* You're in the car rushing because you're always late—*or is that just me?* You've overcommitted yourself once again, and you're wishing you could just drive to the airport and get on the next flight to Maui. *Was that my "outside" voice?* But then I—*I mean you*—turn on the radio and what's that? My/your favorite song is playing! We crank up the music so loud that the millennial in the car at the stoplight next to us grins in approval. Do you see what just happened? We got instantly happy!

Music can make you laugh or cry. It can help ease pain, improve your athletic performance by providing an extra burst of energy, and make you feel happy when you're not. Want to reduce stress? Listen to classical music and meditate. The slower the beat, the more your body relaxes. Soft music is calming and may even improve concentration and sleep, while upbeat music can be energizing.

As a fitness instructor for forty years, I see my students come alive when I play a fast-paced, popular song. It's as if more energy is immediately infused into their bodies—and they smile! There's no question that a biological change takes place when you hear a beautiful melody and lyrics to match.

Listening to music may help speed up recovery after surgery, too. In numerous cases, people in comas have moved their fingers, wiggled their toes, and even smiled when they heard their favorite songs.

Want to be less stressed when driving? Create a traffic playlist of your favorite, happy songs. This might alleviate the anxiety of commuting and keep you from becoming agitated.

Music moves me—literally. In junior high school, I was in the modern dance club. We interpreted lyrics and melodies with our bodies. A slow ballad would include dance movements that were steady and gradual with long, extended arms and legs. As a fitness instructor, I lose myself in the music. When I'm teaching a class, I don't check my cell phone or worry about laundry. I focus on my students, the choreography, and making sure everyone is safe and has fun!

Here are some ideas for times to have playlists:

- while on vacation
- in the dentist's chair
- in traffic
- workouts
- meditation
- relaxing
- while cooking
- while cleaning

Chapter 18
Social Media

*Social media has taken over in America to such an
extreme that to get my own kids to look back a week in
their history is a miracle, let alone 100 years.*
– Steven Spielberg

More than half of us use social media to interact with family and
friends and even strangers. We share personal information
with the world—even with thieves—posting family photos,
travel plans, and our private thoughts. Why? Social media outlets,
such as Facebook, which has over a billion active participants, allow
people to keep in touch with old friends, plan events, sell goods and
services, and get information.

Some of us use it too much. With 114 billion users a month,
Facebook tops the chart of social media giants. It's now apparent
that they sell our personal information to companies interested in
our demographics, but we still log in, every day. Americans aged
eighteen to sixty-four use social media at least an hour a day. What
could you do with seven extra hours a week? It's not likely that we'll
give up social media completely. I mean, we have to check up on our
kids and spouses, right? Would it be possible to shut off your phone
if you knew your kids were safe? I have a friend who makes her kids
hand over their cell phones, laptops, and iPads at ten each night. Who

needs an alert in the middle of the night that Joanie has just changed her relationship status? Not our kids, nor us.

Here's the real tragedy: Texting and using social media while driving causes nearly one-third of all accidents. "Do Not Disturb" apps on most cell phones will send a text message to anyone who calls or texts you, indicating that you're driving and will get back with them as soon as possible. Even better, shut off your phone when you drive; you can always read messages later.

Limit your social media interactions to four minutes today!

Chapter 19
Humor Me

Everything is changing. People are taking their comedians seriously and the politicians as a joke.
– Will Rogers

Are you too serious? At times, we are our worst critics, and that can cause stress and anxiety. Lighten up! Laugh at yourself when you make mistakes. Ever walk out of a public restroom with toilet paper stuck to your shoe? I have. How about attending an important meeting with leftover salad in your teeth? Me too! Have you ever tripped walking up or down stairs? It's all good as long as no one gets hurt! Seriously, little life lessons like these are designed, I believe, to remind us that we need to laugh at ourselves and stop trying to be perfect.

In the forty years I've been teaching group fitness classes in front of tens of thousands, I've taught a dozen classes in which everything went perfectly. Either there's something wrong with the sound system or the lights, or the floor gets slippery because we're all sweating too much, or I get distracted making sure people are safe and mess up the choreography. Here's the clincher—I'm probably the only one who notices!

In one class, I ripped my pants doing squats too low. The show must go on! I tied my sweatshirt around my waist to cover the mishap and finished teaching the class. My students come to get a good workout, and most of them don't really care if we do knee lifts for eight counts or ten. If the misstep is noticeable, I just make a silly face and move on because that's all we can really do in life, isn't it? Certainly, it's important to be aware of our mistakes and learn from them, but often our egos are the only things that get bruised.

Look to your favorite celebrities to see how they handle box office flops: They move on. Everyone makes mistakes. None of us is perfect. In fact, these days, people are looking for transparency. They want to see that people have wrinkles and normal, everyday stress. *New York Times* bestselling author Rachel Hollis posted a photo of her gorgeous body in a bikini—stretch marks and all. It elicited an overwhelmingly positive response.

Life is short. And precious. Have fun. Infuse a bit of comedy in your mistakes, and you might be surprised at how many people will appreciate it.

Chapter 20
Feel

Is it really possible to tell someone else what one feels?
– Leo Tolstoy, *Anna Karenina*

As human beings we become attached to our mothers for comfort, safety, and shelter. The first time we venture away from the warmth of our home and family, we are scared. As we grow older and more independent, we feel adventurous and excited about journeying into the world alone. We all experience love, hate, joy, fear, happiness, peace, anger, and sadness, all emotions critical in helping us determine more about how we want to feel.

Which of those do you want to feel more of more often? Happiness often comes with risk; consider falling in love. Are you willing to take a chance that your heart will be broken, or do you prefer the safer route of staying out of the dating game? Do you really want to feel that tightness in your stomach when you can't pay the rent? It really comes down to how you want to feel. Happy or sad?

Of course, moments in all our lives bring us to our knees, and we just can't seem to get up. After I discovered my husband's affair and love child, I literally thought I was going to die. I *wanted* to die. For days and weeks and months and even years, I experienced moments of regression. I prayed for peace and happiness to come back into my life. My saving grace: I stayed busy, and I had a young son to take care of. Sometimes I had big, dark Jackie O-type sunglasses on while

I made my son a peanut butter and jelly sandwich. I pretended to be the happy mom I once was. Then something happened; eventually I was *happy*. It didn't happen overnight, though. It took years of self-development work and counseling. I had to work on myself, and that didn't seem fair. But you know, it was exactly what I needed to do. I became so much stronger! I no longer tolerate the things I used to. I'm not the meek, people-pleasing person I once was. No, I want to be happy, but that doesn't mean I won't have to deal with difficult situations that will rock my world. We can use the tough stuff to toughen up our stuff.

After reading this book all the way through and completing the journal prompts, you'll better understand why you've endured trials and tribulations. Did failing an exam cause you to study more or to walk a different path? I truly believe that God wanted me to grow, and so those trials were sent to me as a gift. Yep, I said that. Only now, decades later, can I honestly say that I am better off for having endured heartache. That doesn't mean I'm forever immune to it. It was just a hurdle in the track race of life that I needed to jump. More than likely, there will be dozens more for me and for you.

Pray for peace of mind and happiness for yourself and for others. Pray for that feeling you desperately want, and do everything in your power to get there. Avoid the critics as much as possible. They're out there. Satan wants you to be miserable and sad. Surround yourself with positive people and a positive mindset. God will show it to you in His time.

Chapter 21
Last Day

Live as if you were to die tomorrow. Learn as if you were to live forever.
– Mahatma Gandhi

Picture this: I, the woman known for jumping into the splits at a moment's notice, was lying in bed on oxygen, unable to move. After being diagnosed with pre-emphysema from toxic mold poisoning from spores between the walls of my home, I spent a full year recovering with alternative therapies. It seemed as though I'd never get strong enough to teach again and regain my strength. But God had other plans for me! A few years after I was bedridden and unable to walk up a flight of stairs, I became an international Zumba fitness presenter and found my bliss in sharing my love for healthy living with others. Thank you, God.

When you lose your health and are fortunate enough to recover, you know you never want to feel that way again. You eat healthier, exercise more, and become a little more adventurous. My husband asked me to dance onstage—fully clothed, mind you!—at one of his concerts in front of twenty thousand people. I was about to turn fifty. (Why hadn't he asked me when I was thirty or even forty?) Had it not been for my previous life-threatening illness, I don't think I would have agreed to shake my thang onstage at a rock 'n' roll concert. Now

I want to spend the rest of my life doing the things I may never get to do.

It often brings tears to my eyes that I've been given a second chance at life, and I know I don't want to waste it. My problem now is time; there never seems to be enough of it. I desperately want to take every opportunity to smell the roses, watch butterflies, talk with family and friends, and embrace life to the fullest.

What are some of the things you regret missing out on? What if you were to live every day as if it were your last? What would you change?

Chapter 22
Heart Song

Find the thing that makes your heart sing and you'll find your purpose in life.

– Shemane Nugent

n 2003, I was hooked up to an oxygen tank, barely able to walk. Now that I'm healthy again, I travel wherever the music takes me, teaching thousands of fitness instructors and exercise enthusiasts each year. I will continue to do this as long as I can.

Since 1980, I've taught nearly every type of group fitness class: step, Spinning, slide, Body Pump, kickboxing. You name it, and I've probably done it. But nothing moves me as much as Zumba® Fitness does. In one hour, participants dance to more than a dozen songs with different rhythms. Not only am I getting a great workout as the instructor, but the participants are, too. Watching people smile while exercising fills my heart with so much joy!

My focus when teaching a fitness class is to make sure everyone is safe. After one of my rock 'n' roll sessions at an international Zumba convention, a Zumba instructor from Sweden was bent over in the back of the room crying. Worried that she had been injured, I immediately went to her and asked if she was okay. Hearing the music she loved while dancing, she said, had moved her to tears. She smiled and thanked me for the class. No amount of money could equal the way that made me feel. Making a positive difference in others' lives makes my heart sing.

Dig deep inside and listen to that little voice in the back of your mind. You have a gift inside you that is calling you to do something specific. What is your heart song?

Chapter 23
Be a Rock Star

*If you truly believe in your American dream of being
a rock star or, for that matter, a welder, cop, teacher,
landscaper, or anything that is your heart and soul
calling, you must drive yourself to the best of your ability to
be punctual, attentive, professional, kind, friendly, exude
positive energy, and simply be the absolute best that you
can be. Never give up. Work your butt raw 'til you can't
take it anymore, then go for it again, every day.*

– Ted Nugent

We can learn much from men and women talented enough to get up on stage in front of thousands to perform and entertain. They are special; they have power; they *own* the stage. Their presence is commanding.

It takes years, decades even, to cultivate and craft an image and to sustain a successful career. Think about the top dogs: Elvis Presley, the Beatles, the Rolling Stones, Michael Jackson, KISS, Toby Keith, Justin Timberlake, Taylor Swift, Beyoncé, and Bruno Mars, to name a few. What do all those artists have in common? Charisma, confidence, and an incredible work ethic. Their image, their "brand," is carefully crafted. From their hairstyle to the clothes they wear on stage, everything is planned. Who would you be if you were a famous performer? What would you do?

I often hear from people who want to be talented musicians but don't take the necessary time to practice. Good musicians practice their skills over and over until they get it right; then they do it again a hundred times.

So, how does this relate to you? The next time you have a meeting or challenging situation you want to master, rehearse the scenario. Pretend, for a moment, that you're Mick Jagger and own the stage. Rehearse. Rehearse. Then rehearse some more. What will you say and do? Try this: When you walk into a room, be as tall as you can. Posture has a lot to do with presence. Stand up straight and smile!

Chapter 24
Change

Be the change you wish to see in the world.
– Mahatma Gandhi

We experience discontentment for a reason. If you are unhappy or feel unfulfilled in some way, perhaps God is sending you a message to change. Take a look at what still isn't working in your life. Is there a way that those feelings of restlessness can grant you a greater understanding of your life? Be as honest with yourself as you possibly can and reflect on the discord. What would you change about your life, your situation, your environment? Can you take baby steps to get closer to those goals?

You have to buy a lottery ticket to win the lottery. By that I mean you have to move in the direction of change and make an effort before you'll see progress. Do you ever get the feeling that something isn't right but you're just not sure what that is? Stop. Think. Pray. Ask others for input and be open. My mother once told me that if you can't make a decision, that's enough of a decision to make. Don't force a change. Be open to it.

Chapter 25
Pets

Animals are more complete than people. They are wonderful teachers, therapists, and role models for us all.
– Bernie Siegel

Many people feel that their pets are members of their family. Dogs, cats, birds, and even reptiles are included in holiday photos. Astonishingly, some pet owners have bequeathed large sums of money to their pets in their wills. Why all the love and adoration for these furry companions? Dogs are commonly referred to as man's best friend for good reason. No matter how difficult our day is, no matter what we look like or how we feel, our faithful comrades love us unconditionally. Even when we're at our worst—feeling sad, sick, unsightly, and ill or with bed head, baggy sweats, and no makeup—our cherished pals love us. And the feeling is mutual.

Dogs do more than just eat and play. They are essential members of our communities. Dogs comfort the ill and assist the military, law enforcement, and the disabled. Their innate sense of smell helps them detect bad guys, bombs, and drugs, thereby keeping us safe. They can open cupboards and doors and are the eyes for the blind.

Dogs as doctors? You betcha! Dogs can detect cancer, low blood sugar, and seizures.[5] And no matter what kind of mood you're in, your

---

5   www.dogsdetectcancer.org/dogs-detect-cancer-blog/dogs-smell-cancer. See also pets.webmd.com/features/pets-amazing-abilities?page=2

pet is happy to see you and provides unconditional love. Spending time with your pet can help lower blood pressure and cholesterol and prevent heart attacks. Just being around my dogs calms me and boosts my spirit. Pets just want to be loved and to love you back. The happiest part of my day is spending time with my dogs. It diverts my thoughts and puts the focus on what I can do to make them happier and healthier.

If you're not a pet owner, consider volunteering at a shelter. The love you share with those often-abused animals may change their lives and yours.

Chapter 26
Earthing

The art of healing comes from nature, not from the physician. Therefore, the physician must start from nature, with an open mind.

– Paracelsus

Nothing is more peaceful than being surrounded by nature and enveloped by its healing power. The sight of colorful birds and trees, the symphonic sounds of crickets, the gentle kiss of wind on your face, and the smell of freshly cut grass or a fragrant gardenia can be instant stress reducers.

The great outdoors is where we can be alone with our thoughts and feelings. Have you ever gone for a walk to clear your head and suddenly come up with creative thoughts about how to solve a problem or design something new? Inspiration comes in many forms from many places. Being in nature can do more than just enhance your sense of vitality.

When I was hospitalized for migraines, a neurologist suggested I listen to a recording of nature sounds in a dark room. *Why not just go outside?* I wondered. At that point, I realized that breathing fresh air is more than just a temporary fix to relieve stress; it is also innately rewarding for us all. It's energizing and enlightening to fully immerse ourselves in Mother Nature. If you've never watched the sun dip below the horizon, you simply must.

"Earthing" is a new medical term that involves feeling the earth's energy beneath your feet. Rubber- or leather-soled shoes prevent the earth's vibrations from touching your hands or feet. Numerous studies indicate a positive response among those who routinely get in physical touch with the earth. My happiest times are when I'm walking on the beach barefoot. It feels peaceful and rejuvenating, and I always feel healthier.

Want to get more out of your workout? Take it outside! Research shows that exercising outdoors can enhance your self-esteem and lead to a greater sense of well-being.[6]

---

6   pubs.acs.org/doi/abs/10.1021/es903183r

Chapter 27
Friends

The antidote for fifty enemies is one friend.

– Aristotle

My best friend, Nancy, and I met in junior high school. We both liked a boy who was the playa in our school. One week he liked Nancy, and the next week he liked me. Nancy was a top tennis athlete, and, honestly, she scared me. We were on a school ski trip, and, wouldn't you know it, Nancy and I showed up in the same ski outfit! I did everything I could to avoid her. She was waiting in line on the opposite side of the chairlift. As we moved closer to the beginning of the line, I saw that Nancy would be sitting with me. This was it. I was sure she would push me off the lift!

On the twenty-minute ride up the mountain on that cold and snowy night, we eventually started talking and realized that this boy really wasn't a great boyfriend at all. We discovered we had a lot in common. Forty years later, we talk on the phone at least once a day, and Nancy is my son's godmother.

Having a few people with whom you can share your innermost thoughts and complain about your job or spouse and who will lift you up during troubling times is one of the best things you can do to stay happy and healthy. Someone outside your immediate family who knows and loves you can be a great source of advice, too.

Knowing that you can pick up the phone and call someone who will be there in good times and bad can add years to your life.[7]

I still keep in touch with girlfriends I had in high school and college. They know my backstory, and I know theirs. We may see one another only every few years, but it always feels comfortable and cozy to catch up. Recalling memorable events can stimulate brain activity, increase oxygen intake due to laughter, and increase feel-good endorphins, creating a more calm and relaxed feeling.

The emotional and physical value of a vibrant social life is even more important as you age. Friendships often wane as elderly people isolate themselves or watch friends meet the end of their lives. Social interaction can stave off dementia and Alzheimer's and increase life expectancy, according to many studies. Human beings are social creatures. It's natural for us to want to spend time with others who support and uplift us.

7   www.webmd.com/balance/features/good-friends-are-good-for-you

Chapter 28
Giving

We've all experienced dark nights of the soul—times when we endured spiritual crises that brought us to our knees. We lose hope, hit the bottom of the depression pit, and perhaps even consider suicide. Let's be real. Maybe you wouldn't do it, but have you thought about it? I did.

Taking the focus off myself and putting it on others has always lifted me from the deepest, darkest depths of despair. In 2004, Ted, Rocco, and I visited veterans at Brooke Army Medical Center (BAMC) in San Antonio. I can still see and feel that day in my mind.

The three of us went from room to room, floor to floor, visiting severely injured soldiers. The sights were gruesome—much worse than any Hollywood movie could depict. Ted played his guitar and entertained some of the troops in a rehab room. A young man who had suffered serious burns all over his body was strapped onto a bed; his arms and legs were extended. Emblazoned in my memory are the moaning sounds he made while his limbs were stretched so that new skin would have a chance to grow.

As we ascended to higher floors, the conditions of these hero warriors worsened.

The cheery demeanor of a beautiful, dark-haired woman overpowered the fact that half of her face had been maimed. She wore a wide and bright smile as she talked about recovering quickly so she could rejoin her fellow soldiers.

Nineteen-year-old Corporal John Chrzanowski had been brought in the night before we arrived. Wrapped from head to toe like a mummy, John had been burned all over. To minimize the chance for infection, his visitors were kept to a minimum. Ted scrubbed up, put on a facemask and gown, and headed in to give John a pep talk. Rocco and I stood outside the room with John's mother, Nancy. I had no idea what to say to her. How could any words bring her comfort? I asked if there was anything she needed, anything I could do for her. With all the confidence in the world that her son would someday make a full recovery, Nancy Chrzanowski lifted her chin and said defiantly that her son was an outdoorsman and she couldn't imagine him recovering without being able to get outside. At the time, there was no patio at BAMC to shelter burned and wounded veterans from direct sunlight.

Nancy's words slightly stunned me, but I leaped into the conversation as if something had taken over my words. I had zero experience with fundraising and no idea how I would do it, but I told Nancy I'd raise the money for a patio at the center so that her son and so many others could get outside into fresh air but stay out of the sun. With the help of my husband, Governor Rick Perry of Texas, and so many others, a beautiful pavilion was created at BAMC and has provided relief to hundreds of deserving and honored American military veterans. That experience prompted me to get involved in charities like Operation Finally Home and K9s for Warriors to help wounded soldiers and their families. Most recently, we raised money to provide a track chair to a veteran who had lost his legs. Now, he can go to the beach with his family and not worry about the complications of walking with prosthetic legs in the sand.

Every year, Ted and I are involved in dozens and dozens of charity events. We've hosted too many children with terminal illnesses for me to count. Or want to count. Meeting innocent children stricken by a death warrant is heartbreaking. It's so unfair to them and their families. It seems to put everything in perspective. How dare I complain of having a bad hair day or gaining a few pounds? Those children would love to have my problems. So whenever I have my pity days, I think about people who struggle with much more daunting tribulations, and I get involved.

You don't have to write a check to make a difference. One Thanksgiving, Ted, Rocco, and I visited a soup kitchen and served the homeless. Lend a helping hand to others, and you'll be more appreciative of what you have.

Chapter 29
Intuition

The only real valuable thing is intuition.
– Albert Einstein

ave you ever had a gut feeling about a person or a situation? By "gut feeling," I mean inner wisdom, the power of your feelings in your body, not logical thinking. This is a gray area of metaphysical science that has recently gained popularity among doctors and psychologists, although philosophers such as Aristotle, Plato, Jung, and many more have discussed it for centuries.

Unless you've studied philosophy or metaphysics or there is someone in your life who has encouraged you to trust your intuition, it's unlikely you've had the confidence to learn from or even listen to your instincts. Some think it's a wishy-washy approach to making a judgment call and can't be trusted. With modern technology, we rely more on cold, hard facts and statistics than our gut feelings about something or someone. But have you ever met someone and instantly liked or disliked them? You can't describe exactly why you had that feeling, but you did. That's intuitive thinking, and it serves people well. Law enforcement, the military, and athletes use intuition to direct their actions.

Today's challenge is an important one. Our instincts can be a very reliable source for decision making if we allow ourselves to embrace our gut feelings. We may feel pulled to do or not do something, and that inner knowing may save our lives; for example, we might take a different route to work, only to find out an accident occurred on our usual path, or we may simply have second thoughts about a person that we cannot corroborate.

For at least four minutes today, trust everything your intuition tells you.

Chapter 30
The Enneagram

The Enneagram is a tool that awakens our compassion
for people just as they are, not the people we wish they
would become so our lives would become easier.
- Ian Morgan Cron

T he Enneagram is an important guide to understanding and
accepting our behavior, and it helps explain why some people
just seem to push our buttons. With a history dating back to
the 1500s and Christian roots, the Enneagram is a personality typing
system identifying childhood wounds that prevent us from living
authentically as adults. These survival mechanisms once served us
as self-preservation tools to combat bullies, to be loved, or to get
attention. Carrying those behaviors into our adult years, however,
can cause us to be frustrated and resentful because we mask who we
really are at our core. Being the good little girl or boy who constantly
tries to please others can get exhausting. Trust me. We cover wounds
that are buried deep in our souls with happy faces, when in reality
we are screaming inside. We camouflage our innermost thoughts
so that we can appear to be in control. Have you ever shoved dirty
laundry, random socks, or toys into a closet before visitors arrived
to make it appear as if you have the perfect home *and life*? At times,
we all portray an image of what we think others expect of us, while

sacrificing what we know deep in our hearts does not resonate with our souls. Then we wonder why we're not happy.

In his book, *The Essential Enneagram*, Christopher Heuertz describes the Enneagram as: ". . . nine ways we lie to ourselves about who we think we are, nine ways we can come clean about those illusions, and nine ways we can find our way back to God."

See if you can find yourself in the nine different Enneagram types:

- the peacemaker
- the perfectionist
- the helper
- the performer
- the romantic
- the investigator
- the loyalist
- the enthusiast
- the challenger

There are also twenty-seven sub-types that reflect who you are when you are at your best (happiest) and your worst (furious). Like looking through a kaleidoscope and seeing the same image in a different lens, the Enneagram has the power to heal deep wounds and resolve conflicts if we can subtly shift the focus. It is both a rude awakening and enlightening tool for those looking to live more authentically.

Corporations such as Best Buy and Avon use the Enneagram to bridge communications with employees. The CIA uses it to understand more about individuals on their watch list. The Vatican is even getting in on the action.[8] The Enneagram has helped me to better understand more about myself and why others react differently

---

8   https://www.newsweek.com/find-self-take-number-188156

to the same situations. It has opened my eyes so intensely that when someone disagrees with me, instead of instinctively reacting with anger, I softly smile. I get it. Each of us is doing the best we can with the information and childhood wounds we've experienced.

Chapter 31
Smile

Smile. It will either warm their hearts or piss them off.
Either way, you win!
– Author Unknown

When I was working at a radio station in Detroit as the traffic reporter, a coworker seemed to snarl at me whenever we crossed paths. One day, I finally asked her if I'd done anything to upset her. "I just have a problem with people who walk around smiling for no reason," she said. Well, I have good reason to smile. I'm truly grateful for my blessings. What I want most out of life is peace of mind, health, and happiness. So, when I have those three things, why wouldn't I smile? Wouldn't the world be a better place if we all walked around smiling and content?

Once, on a brutally hot and humid day in Miami, Rocco and I were shopping and sightseeing. We stopped into a convenience store to get a cold drink. The building was decrepit, and it seemed to be hotter inside than it was outside, but we were tired and thirsty. The clerk, with a broad smile and cheery demeanor, greeted us with a confident, "Hello, my friends!" His happy attitude was contagious. We immediately smiled through our sweat, bought some cold drinks, and thanked the man for being so happy. We walked back to our hotel with a spring in our step.

Why do some people always seem to have a chip on their shoulder while others are grateful to have shoulders? Negative thoughts often enter our minds throughout the day. Whether it's the guy who cut us off in traffic or bad news, our journeys on Earth are emotional roller-coaster rides. Although that man in the convenience store had a minimum-wage job and worked in conditions that were less than desirable, he was pleasant and upbeat. Being happy is a choice, one that can trigger a chain reaction for the people you encounter.

Chapter 32
Expression

Unexpressed emotions will never die. They are buried alive and will come forth later in uglier ways.

– Sigmund Freud

s an emotion or idea bottled up inside you? Has your soul been craving something more or something different? Do you have a yearning to take a trip, volunteer for a charity, change careers, get married or divorced, sing or dance, climb a mountain, or just relax? Give your mind time to explore the possibilities. Take this blank space to draw or write about your current feelings.

Part II
—
Healthy Mind Journal

Perhaps you've always been a risk-taker and now you want to be more secure. It doesn't matter. Knowing what you know right now, knowing that you are wise enough to comprehend exactly what you want in your life's journey, spend four minutes writing down exactly how you *want* to feel.

_____
_____
_____
_____
_____
_____
_____
_____

If you had four days to live, what would you do?

_____
_____
_____
_____
_____

Just as important, what wouldn't you do?

_____
_____
_____
_____
_____

What is your gift? What makes your heart sing?

_____

_____

_____

_____

_____

_____

_____

_____

_____

_____

_____

How can you incorporate that activity into your busy life more often?

_____

_____

_____

_____

_____

_____

Create your rocking brand/image here.

_____

_____

_____

_____

_____

_____

What lessons do you think you can learn from your feelings of discontentment?

_____

_____

_____

_____

_____

_____

What is your favorite type of pet? A dog? Cat? Bird? Spend a few minutes writing something about a pet that has been meaningful to you and why.

_____

_____

_____

_____

_____

_____

Spend four minutes Earthing, walking on grass, getting your hands in the dirt, or (if it's cold) feeling the frozen ground. What sensation(s) do you feel?

_____

_____

_____

_____

_____

_____

_____

We all are drawn to nature in some way. Use this space to describe your favorite experiences in the great outdoors.

_____

_____

_____

_____

_____

_____

_____

_____

_____

_____

_____

_____

Write about your closest friend and what that friendship means to you.

_____

_____

_____

_____

_____

_____

_____

_____

_____

_____

_____

_____

What can you do to help someone today? This week?

_____
_____
_____
_____
_____

Can you recall a few times that your intuition served you well? Why or why not?

_____
_____
_____
_____
_____
_____

What are some negative thoughts that reoccur most often in your life?

_____
_____
_____
_____
_____
_____
_____
_____
_____
_____
_____

What can you do or think about to drive those thoughts away?

_____

_____

_____

_____

_____

_____

Take four minutes to draw, color, make shapes, write down words, get angry, or be happy—whatever floats your boat. Create from the heart. Go!

_____

_____

_____

_____

_____

_____

Spend four minutes writing or drawing pictures about what your dream life looks like.

Think of a few things that bring you so much joy, compassion, confidence, and peace that your heart feels like it will explode: A smiling baby, a vast sky, the ocean, a puppy or kitten. Imagine the capacity to feel those emotions during challenging times—in your deepest, darkest moments of fear and vulnerability. How would that change your life?

Now, take your four minutes of positive action and examine the things that bring you profound joy. Grab your pen and start writing about what makes you happy. Dig deep, and don't just focus on the obvious.

What makes you happy?

_____
_____
_____
_____
_____
_____
_____
_____
_____
_____
_____
_____
_____
_____
_____
_____
_____
_____
_____
_____
_____
_____
_____
_____
_____
_____
_____

A Course in Miracles states, "Depression always arises ultimately from a sense of being deprived of something you want and do not have."[9] What caused your deepest depression and sadness?

Pretend, for a moment, that you are your own therapist. What lesson can you learn from your grief? Is there some sort of silver lining, something that has prompted you to be more thoughtful or caring to yourself or others because of tragedy?

_____

_____

_____

_____

_____

_____

_____

It's time to take action. Describe your purpose in life.

_____

_____

_____

_____

_____

_____

_____

_____

_____

_____

_____

9   *A Course in Miracles*; White Crow Books, 2012

Write down your most important morals (being honest, kind, etc.) and
how you display them.

_____

_____

_____

_____

_____

_____

What do you value most? Friends, family, or money?

_____

_____

_____

_____

_____

_____

None of us is perfect; we all make mistakes. What can you do to stay
on course with your own set of morals and values?

_____

_____

_____

_____

_____

_____

_____

_____

_____

_____

_____

_____

If you haven't been lovey-dovey with anyone or expressed yourself freely, start now. It can be difficult at first, but you'll never be sorry you did it. Who are the people you love most? Write about them here.

_____

_____

_____

_____

_____

_____

_____

_____

_____

_____

Take a look at the percentage of time you spend on various activities now and then in sixty days. Write down the percentage of time you spend on each activity.

- work (including business seminars/meetings):
- family (including kids' activities):
- exercise (including play/free time):
- meditation/spirituality/religion:

Review these percentages in thirty days. Write down what has changed and why.

_____

_____

_____

_____

_____

_____

What are some of the risks you've taken but failed at?

_____
_____
_____
_____
_____
_____

What have you learned from those ventures?

_____
_____
_____
_____
_____

Describe a time when you took a risk and were successful.

_____
_____
_____
_____
_____

How did you feel when your failure turned into triumph?

_____
_____
_____
_____
_____

How can you apply what you've learned to another opportunity?

_____

_____

_____

_____

_____

What are a few errands or responsibilities on your to-do list that you haven't checked off?

_____

_____

_____

_____

_____

What activities will you give up this week to complete more important business?

_____

_____

_____

_____

_____

_____

What paperwork or errands have you been avoiding?

_____

_____

_____

_____

_____

_____

At what time and day will you complete those tasks?

_____

_____

Be honest when answering these questions. If this were the last day of your life and if you had a choice, what would you do if you could change your occupation without repercussions?

_____

_____

_____

_____

_____

_____

_____

_____

_____

_____

_____

_____

Is there something you've always wanted to do but were too afraid to try?

_____

_____

_____

_____

_____

What's your dream job?

_____

_____

_____

_____

_____

_____

Can you take small steps toward living that dream without losing your current job and insurance and uprooting your family? What attainable steps can you take toward having your dream job (for instance, working from home, getting up earlier, going to bed later)?

_____

_____

_____

_____

_____

_____

What would it be like to live out your dream and have a different, more exciting career?

_____

_____

_____

_____

_____

_____

While there are a million get-rich-quick schemes, few of them work. So let's explore a few ideas on how you can make more money doing the things you love to do—the real American dream. Be as straightforward here as possible.

What do you love to do?

_____
_____
_____
_____
_____
_____
_____

What skills do you have?

_____
_____
_____
_____
_____
_____
_____

Have you ever thought of a way to improve a product or service?

_____
_____
_____
_____
_____
_____
_____

How can you combine what you love to do with your skills and improve or create a product?

_____

_____

_____

_____

_____

_____

What can you do above and beyond your call of duty in your work or home life?

_____

_____

_____

_____

_____

_____

Who is someone in authority you've always wanted to contact?

_____

_____

_____

_____

What would you like to tell him or her?

_____

_____

_____

_____

_____

_____

Spend four minutes today unplugging household items that aren't in immediate use. What did you unplug today? Where else can you save energy?

_____

_____

_____

_____

_____

_____

_____

List the steps you'd like to take in any disaster (grabbing important papers or having a ready list of phone numbers, including Red Cross and disaster relief numbers, etc.).

_____

_____

_____

_____

_____

_____

_____

What have you always wanted to learn more about?

_____

_____

_____

_____

_____

_____

What language(s) would you like to learn?

_____

_____

Start now. For four minutes, learn a couple of words in another language. Write them down here. Track your progress in thirty days.

_____

_____

_____

_____

_____

_____

Have you ever thought of taking an exotic trip to Fiji or skiing the Alps, even if it's next year or five years from now? Where do you want to go?

_____

_____

_____

_____

_____

_____

When do you want to go? (Or when can you go?)

_____

_____

_____

_____

_____

Who's in your travel party?

_____
_____
_____
_____
_____
_____
_____

What do you want to see most on your journey?

_____
_____
_____
_____
_____
_____
_____

List the expenses for this trip:

_____
_____
_____
_____
_____
_____
_____
_____

What unnecessary spending can you reduce between now and the time of your trip?

_____

_____

_____

_____

_____

_____

_____

Spend four minutes writing down a playlist of upbeat, happy songs to motivate you through a tough workout and to uplift you when you're feeling blue. Or write down calmer, softer songs for stretching and meditation exercises.

_____

_____

_____

_____

_____

_____

_____

_____

Why do you like to use social media?

_____

_____

_____

_____

_____

Does it ever negatively impact you or your family?

_____

_____

_____

_____

_____

_____

_____

Write a little bit about how you can slow down in your life.

_____

_____

_____

_____

_____

_____

_____

Write down a few funny things you've done that didn't go as planned but made you smile. Identifying silly behavior is a great way to find positive things to think about when negative thoughts come up. Replace the negative thoughts with thoughts that make you laugh!

_____

_____

_____

_____

_____

_____

_____

_____

Part III

A Healthy Body

Chapter 33
Your Body

*Take care of your body. It's the only
place you have to live.*

- Jim Rohn

This is the part where we talk about the tough stuff; it's also most likely the content that made you pick up this book. With 50 percent of Americans overweight and 30 percent obese, maybe you're looking for a realistic approach to getting in shape once and for all. Or maybe you've reached menopause, and, well, some things have gone south. If you want to make any changes in your physique, it's time to get real.

Here goes . . .

Look at yourself in the mirror in just your undies. Do you have a little *somethin' somethin'* hanging over the top of your panties? *Do we still call it a muffin top?* Do you have tricep flab that waves back at you? How about cellulite? *I know, girl. I know.* The other day I was trying on clothes in a department store dressing room that had the kind of mirror that told the truth, not the kind that made you look two sizes smaller. I knew my eyes had been getting worse, but when I looked closer . . . *um . . . yep. I have cellulite, too, sister!* And yes, the tricep wave is my specialty. I'm a flapper. Coming face-to-face with the truth can be incredibly motivating, while putting clothes on just covers the problem, doesn't it?

I've dedicated my life not just to staying in shape but also to being healthy. As a group fitness instructor, I've taught more than six thousand classes and shared my passion for healthy living with tens of thousands. I trained with Spinning creator Johnny G, and developed Zumba® in the Circuit with Beto Perez, the creator of Zumba®. I've trained thousands of fitness instructors in Sydney, Paris, London, and nearly every state in the United States. I owned my own aerobics studio, and as I mentioned earlier, I was once named Detroit's Most Physical Female. (Okay, so that contest was held in a bar, but I won!)

The point is, I know all about physical fitness. So you'd think I'd have photoshoot-ready six-pack abs. *Um . . . nope. I don't.* And I don't always eat 100 percent clean—more like 80 percent. After all, I like Fritos! And cupcakes. And chips and guacamole. *Should I go on?* I don't know about you, but I'm not giving up my favorite foods for the rest of my life. On the other hand, I don't want to be disgusted by what I see, *or just saw*, in the mirror.

So, if you're with me, let's get to the *meat* of the matter. Let's get this party started and get our rears in gear, shall we? Here's where to start:

1. Weigh yourself and take your measurements. Are you content with the numbers? Do you want to look better and feel better? Have no fear! Rome wasn't built in a day, and you didn't get that body overnight.

2. Consult with your physician before starting any diet or exercise program.

3. Keep a food journal, starting now. Write down the foods that make you feel lighter and more energetic. Do you ever feel tired after a meal? Write down what you ate. How about food that makes you go *boom?*

4. Which exercises do you like, and which will you never, ever even try? Make a list.

Chapter 34

Fitness: What You Need to Know

Nothing lifts me out of a bad mood better than a hard workout on my treadmill. It never fails. Exercise is nothing short of a miracle.

– Cher

n high school, I was thirty pounds heavier than I am now. Then in college, I became part of the Freshman Fifteen Club—not a club you want to join. At a time when I should have been at peak physical condition, I was overweight. If I add it all up, I've gained and lost over a hundred pounds in my life.

As a smart college girl, I knew many ways to lose weight. The all-time worst weight-loss gimmicks included wrapping my body in plastic, donning a sweat suit, sitting in the sauna, and simply starving myself. None of this, as you probably know, worked. Only when I started to teach group fitness classes regularly did I shed pounds.

Exercise is the key to lifelong health; it lowers your blood pressure, helps you sleep better, prevents inflammation (which can cause diseases such as cancer), and works wonders to reduce stress. Some days, you may want to run a marathon or swim a mile, and some days, you may just want to go for a walk or do some stretches.

So how do you get in shape and look great as quickly and painlessly as possible? The workout crazes that come along every year feed that frenzy, but as a fitness professional for forty years (and counting), I've seen 'em come and go. Many are terrific, but you actually have to do them!

Having trained in dozens of fitness programs, from step to spinning to kickboxing, I appreciate the value of each curriculum and enjoy most of them. I love to dance but don't have hours every day to get my heart pumping *and* do strength training. I know I can get a full-body workout in sixty minutes and have a blast by combining fitness with dance (Zumba in the Circuit). Am I biased? You better believe it! I've spent hundreds of hours training, testing, and trying different fitness modalities and have learned that an interval training fitness program is the most effective. Try some cardio, like dancing to one of your favorite songs. Then, for the next song, do exercises targeted to a specific area, such as squats and lunges for legs. Repeat the process until you've worked every major muscle group and you're sweating.

Once you get started on one specific exercise program, your body can become used to it. As a survival mechanism, your body is equipped with the resources to adapt to physical stress. It will eventually adjust to the impact from whatever exercises you do regularly. You'll most likely reach a plateau where you may not see any changes. This is called the principle of adaptation. To continually progress and break through that adaptation phase, you have to use your muscles in a different way. Here's how:

1. Increase the intensity, frequency, and duration of your workouts. For example, if you like to walk, walk faster for four minutes. Pick up the pace. To increase the frequency, walk more often. Instead of just three times a week, strive for five. Then, lengthen the time you move from ten or twenty

minutes at a time to forty or sixty. Add some lunges or jumps to increase the intensity. Mix it up!

2. Find the thing that makes your heart sing, and you'll do it more often—and have fun! You'll be more interested in exercising if you like what you're doing. Some people prefer weight training, running, swimming, biking, or yoga. I like to do all those activities, and I vary my workouts often. It's best to utilize your muscles in different ways to achieve a well-rounded fitness program and a balanced body.

3. Get out! You don't have to buy DVDs or gym memberships. Go for a walk, take the stairs, and park your car farther from the door.

4. Exercise at least twenty minutes, three days per week. *At least.*

5. Join the club. A sedentary lifestyle will contribute to weight gain and muscle loss. Millions pay for health club memberships, yet a majority go unused. Working out in a group setting motivates me. I'm less likely to quit my work out early, answer my cell phone, or get distracted, but some people enjoy exercising in the convenience of their own homes at the time they choose. Options are great!

Chapter 35
4-Minute Exercises

An early-morning walk is a blessing for the whole day.
– Henry David Thoreau

G etting regular exercise doesn't mean you have to work out an hour or more a day. Who has time for that? Short bursts of strength-training moves and at least three days of cardiovascular exercise weekly can help you stay fit. Many of us use the lack of time as an excuse not to exercise. If I'm not teaching a fitness class, I can come up with more excuses than anybody about why I'm too busy to exercise. Laundry, cooking, cleaning, etc. Life gets in the way, right? Wrong!

Starting now, make exercising a priority. You make time to do the things you really want or have to do. Try this: Schedule time with *yourself* in your calendar at least three times a week for a minimum of thirty minutes. Set the alarm. Get your exercise clothes ready the night before. Go to the gym, find an on-line workout program, go for a walk, or dance around at home—it doesn't matter. Program a daily four-minute workout reminder! You'll be amazed at the results from four minutes of squats and push-ups.

Here are a few exercises that will tone you up in four minutes. Stop whatever you're doing (unless you're breast feeding, sitting in a doctor's office, at church, etc.), and do four minutes of push-ups, sit-ups, squats, and burpees. Go to exhaustion on one exercise and then switch.

Push-ups

1. Place your hands a little more than shoulder width apart.
2. You can be on your toes or your knees.
3. Keep your head in a neutral position.
4. Tighten your abdominals.
5. Lower your body until your chest reaches the floor.

Sit-ups

1. Lie on your back with your knees bent and your lower back pressing against the floor. Pull in your abdominals.
2. Keep your hands behind your head to support your neck and back while lifting your chest toward the ceiling, moving only a couple of inches.
3. Try to keep shoulders off the ground.

Squats

Sitting on a plane during a five-hour cross-country trip, I heard flight attendants counting to twenty; then there would be silence, and they would walk around the cabin assisting passengers. I'd hear them counting again to twenty; then it would stop. They were behind the galley walls, so I couldn't see what they were doing. I just happened to get up to go to the restroom while they were counting. (That's not entirely true. I had *totally* planned it!) They were doing squats! Twenty squats, five times throughout the flight, equaled one hundred squats. Kudos to those flight attendants for creating a healthy work environment.

Squats done properly can improve your health by jump-starting your metabolism. They engage the body's largest muscle group and require oxygen intake, which speeds up the metabolic waste expulsion. Squats help with balance and are the best exercises to tighten and tone the lower body.

Here are a few tips to do squats properly:

1. Stand with your feet shoulder-width apart.
2. Keep your back in a neutral position, and keep your knees centered over your feet.
3. Slowly bend your knees. Look in a side mirror to make sure your knees stay centered over your feet while you press your hips toward the back of the room.
4. Lower your hips as if you were about to sit in a chair.

Try doing four minutes of squats today and at least once a week. Check your progress in sixty days!

Burpees and Kicks

Burpees are quick exercises that incorporate muscles over the entire body, are great cardiovascular workouts, and are used to train the military and top athletes. Consult a physician before starting any exercise program. Never heard of them? Allow me to introduce you.

How to do a burpee:

1. Stand up straight, squat, and place your hands on the floor in front of you.
2. Shoot your feet back so you're in a plank position.
3. Drop your chest to the floor and do a push-up.
4. Pull your feet back up into a squat position.
5. Jump up as high as you can.

Kicks work the abdominals, or the core, as well as the glutes, quadriceps, and hamstrings.

Chapter 36
Play

You will find more happiness growing down than up.
– Unknown

There's more to playing than just having fun, though that's important, too! Many of us are just too serious. We seldom have laugh-out-loud fun. Playtime helps us physically and mentally by allowing us to exercise and be creative. A childlike recess can stimulate our imaginations. Physical exercise can release hormones that create euphoria, similar to the process that occurs during sex. These hormones also block pain.

On top of it all, having fun burns calories and helps us temporarily ignore our troubles.

Even at the ripe old age of fifty-seven, if there's a trampoline nearby, I'm on it! When Rocco was growing up, I was the parent who was down on her knees crawling through the hamster-wheel-like play centers. First of all, I wanted to keep an eye on him, but it was also too much darn fun.

Here are a few things you can do to play for four minutes today:

- Turn on music and dance.
- Go to a park and climb on the monkey bars.
- Play with your dog.
- Ride a bike.
- Jump on a trampoline.

Chapter 37
What Am I Supposed to Eat?

Let food be thy medicine; thy medicine shall be thy food.
– Hippocrates

have a confession to make: I didn't always eat healthy. As a teen, I ate fast food every day. In high school and college, I was thirty pounds heavier than I am now. Though we had fancy dinners with crystal and china every Sunday after church, we were often served Hamburger Helper, chicken pot pies, and frozen dinners. During junior high and high school, I would frequently have a peanut butter and jelly sandwich, a bag of chips, and two Hostess cupcakes for lunch. I was involved in many sports and sometimes called "healthy" or "big-boned." Growing up, my nickname was Shelly, and occasionally, kids called me "Shelly with the big, fat belly." I prayed that I would one day be as skinny as the models on magazine covers.

In my twenties, I finally started to understand how food affects our bodies and that I needed to give up the junk food. Exercise and healthy eating are responsible for overall health and wellness. Yes, genetics plays a role. I'll never be five eleven and a hundred and ten. For one thing, I like to eat. But I've figured out how to maintain my body weight and size by eliminating a few things from the list below. I can still eat foods I crave like cupcakes and cookies in moderation. This, however, is not a one-size-fits-all nutrition plan.

It's important for everyone to become their own investigative sleuth. What's best for my body might not be best for you. Talk to your doctor, get a food allergy test, and keep a food journal. All our bodies are unique with a completely different genetic make-up. It's no wonder that a universal nutrition plan doesn't work for everyone.

Some of us may have tried diet programs but quit. Who remembers the cookie diet? There seems to be a new, improved way to eat every year. Milk does your body good—until it doesn't. Diets don't work because there's either too much preparation or they're impossible to maintain. It has to be a lifestyle change, one that's realistic and manageable.

I'm a believer in moderation. As I mentioned, I've tried a lot of diets, not just to lose weight but also to feel better. Eighty percent of what I eat is clean. Most of the time, I don't use sauces or eat fried food, soda, candy, cakes, etc. Notice that I said "most of the time." I believe that life is worth living to the fullest and that means enjoying your favorite foods *in moderation.*

At the least, you should:

- Avoid white bread, white flour, and white sugar.
- Avoid sugary soft drinks and too much fruit juice.
- Avoid gluten-heavy ingredients.
- Avoid food dyes.
- Avoid chips and candy.
- Eliminate processed food.
- Minimize deli-style meat that contains nitrates.
- Become a label reader—get to know what's in your food.
- Make smart choices at the grocery store—if it's not in your house, you can't eat it.
- Hydrate your body by drinking half of your body weight in ounces of filtered water.

Another important change to make: Stop thinking about what you're going to have for lunch while eating breakfast. Keep busy. Doing something you love prevents you from eating out of boredom. Have you ever been so involved in a project that you forgot to eat? Compare that to inhaling a bag of chips while watching television.

Healthy snacks:

- Cut vegetables and hummus
- Air-popped popcorn with a drizzle of olive oil and salt
- A large lettuce leaf as a wrap (instead of a tortilla)
- Celery or apples and nut butter
- Whole, natural nuts

So, what should you eat? Whatever works best for you. Listen to your body. If you resonate with a vegetarian diet, that's cool. We should all add more greens. You shouldn't feel pressured to succumb to the latest weight-loss plan. Personally, I don't eat a lot of chicken, pork or red meat because of the way it makes my body feel. I have more energy and feel lightest when I eat mostly vegetables and fish. Check out the Resources section in the back of the book for a sample of what I eat each day.

Chapter 38
How to Eat Mindfully

*You can tell a lot about a fellow's character
by his way of eating jellybeans.*
– Ronald Reagan

Most of us eat too quickly. If you've ever eaten fast food while driving, you know what I mean. Maybe you sat in front of the TV with a bag of chips and later realized you've inhaled the whole bag. I have. Does it seem to you as though some people eat slowly? Perhaps you're a fast eater. People who eat quickly consume more calories, are typically overweight, and likely have digestive problems.

Eating slowly makes you appreciate food and become more mindful of its taste, quality, and texture. Eating slowly also helps you digest the meal better and promotes healthy living and less stress. Considering our stress-filled, hectic lifestyles, we should slow down when eating, engage in conversation more, and be mindful of each bite. Try it. You might like it!

Chapter 39
Body Appreciation

*Health is the result of relinquishing all attempts
to use the body lovelessly.*

– A Course in Miracles, Foundation for Inner Peace

Before you get too absorbed in getting the perfect physique, understand this: I love you just the way you are, and I want you to be the healthiest, happiest version of you. This book in no way is meant to body shame anyone. I encourage you not to get discouraged about your size, shape, or tricep waves; rather, accept who you are and how you look, but always strive to be the healthiest version of *you* possible. There's someone out there who would give anything to have your body, cellulite and all. My friend and fellow Zumba instructor Corina Gutierrez is a special lady with an important message just for you:

> *I was born with a brittle bone condition called osteogenesis imperfecta (OI). I am three feet tall, and I use a motorized wheelchair to get around. I also have severe scoliosis, restricted lung disease, and asthma.*
>
> *Growing up, I had to overcome many health and identity issues. I was born weighing four pounds with*

a heart murmur, a fractured arm and leg, dislocated hip and shoulder, and two broken ribs. Doctors did not expect me to live very long. I literally lived in and out of the hospital for the past eight years of my life due to fractures, surgeries, and respiratory issues.

Four years ago, I began doing a dance fitness program called Zumba that improved my health in more ways than I or anyone thought possible! It increased my self-confidence. I grew an inch because my muscles stretched out, and my breathing, range of motion in my arms and legs, and my strength all improved a great deal. All these wonderful improvements with my own health inspired me to become a Zumba fitness instructor to help others in similar situations. It took me a while, but I realized I was here to bring hope to the hopeless. God has given me His heart to love the unlovable. He has given me knowledge and wisdom to share with the world to help people walk in their purpose.

Many people look at me and think that the biggest disability one could have is the inability to walk, but the biggest disability one could have is not walking in your purpose.

Chapter 40

The Mind/Body Connection

Wellness is the complete integration of body, mind, and spirit—the realization that everything we do, think, feel, and believe has an effect on our state of well-being.

– Greg Anderson

Being healthy and happy is based not only on what we eat and how we exercise but also on how we think and feel. Scientists are discovering how our emotions affect our health. We've all heard stories about couples that have been together for a long time, and after one of them died, the other soon followed, although he or she had no terminal health problems. Broken Heart Syndrome is real.

If you experience negative emotions from the loss of a loved one, depression, or a physical illness, you might find some relief with meditation, relaxation, and finding things to distract you during difficult times. When weekly debilitating migraines left me bedridden and nothing—not even prescription drugs—would abort the pain, I tried an unconventional meditation exercise that brought relief. Let's try it together:

> Close your eyes. Picture what that pain looks like in your mind's eye. Give it a shape, a color (something dark), and even a name. Take several long, deep breaths. With your eyes still closed, picture the air

coming into your lungs as a bright color. Watch it spread throughout your body. Repeat several times until you begin to feel the tension in your neck and shoulders relax. Imagine the dark color and shape of the thing you called pain is exhaled. Soon, your body will become a brighter, healthier, more vivacious color that takes over the pain.

We live in a world that exposes us to way too much information. Take a look at network or cable news programs; watch the constant news ticker running with breaking stories while the newscaster is interjecting information. Note the station logo in the corner and the backdrop of moving designs. Unfortunately, we have become used to information overload; we need to be still and listen to the messages our bodies are communicating.

Studies show that we can lower blood pressure, the risk of heart attacks and strokes, and diminish anxiety just by being still and calming our bodies and minds. Meditation helps the mind find a happy ground where it's not working so hard. It helps control anxious and negative thoughts. When we are happy, we function at a healthier, more efficient rate, which causes less strain on our organs and more peace of mind.

Chapter 41
Stress

*Who of you by worrying could add
a single hour to his life?*
– Luke 12:25

n the previous chapter, we talked about the effect negative emotions have on the body. Some of us take on unwarranted anxiety. We're a nation—a world—of overachievers; we do too much, and we think too much. In this highly advanced technological age, it's normal to multitask—driving and talking on the phone; walking and texting; or even driving, texting, and talking. That has to stop. Not only is it dangerous, since distracted driving causes many accidents, it's also unhealthy.

Like carrying a heavy suitcase, stress and negative emotions can weigh us down. We add more and more things to our to-do lists and then wonder why we don't feel good. How much can you stuff in that suitcase, girl? Isn't it getting heavy?

What can you do? In the pockets of your time, focus only on you. Do you hold tension in your neck, shoulders, or abdomen? See if this helps: Close your eyes, put your hand on your chest, and feel your heartbeat. Focus on slowing down your breath and relaxing every part of your body, beginning at your head, down through your jaw, shoulders, chest, arms, legs, and toes. Imagine that every cell is operating at its utmost potential. Envision every muscle and bone healthy and strong.

Bring your awareness to your breath. Pretend you're breathing through a straw slowly. Inhale to the count of ten and exhale even more slowly. Try to slow your heartbeat. Listen to your surroundings and allow yourself to let go of the tension.

In one of my favorite movies, *The Last Samurai*, a samurai warrior teaches Tom Cruise's character (Nathan) how to fight with a sword, but he also shares life lessons about overthinking. Here's the conversation:

> Warrior: Please forgive. Too many mind[s].
> Nathan (Tom): Too many mind?
> Warrior: Mind sword, mind people watch, mind enemy.

Our minds can become the enemy when we overthink. We try to do everything and to please everyone (or is that just me?). Living life more slowly and mindfully will improve your focus and attention and reduce your heart rate, blood pressure, and risk of stroke. Slowing down helps you appreciate the simple things and all the things with which you're blessed. Never miss a chance to smell the flowers. Just for today, do things with more kindness and grace.

- Turn off your cell phone for at least a couple of hours a day.
- Take a deep breath and count to four when you're about to explode.
- Don't take your loved ones for granted.
- Stop and smell the flowers.
- Look at the starry night sky.
- Be a better listener.

Chapter 42
Mold

M old can be a toxic and dangerous living substance that thrives in damp and dark environments. A common misconception exists that mold only grows in certain geographic locations. The truth is, mold can grow anywhere that has a porous substance, water infiltration, and lack of ventilation. It grew between the walls of our home. We never saw anything. We just kept getting sicker and sicker. (If you skipped the Introduction, now's a good time to read it and hear my story. It's why I wrote this book.)

Mold can grow in your home, office, and your car. While there are thousands of types of molds, several are highly toxic and can cause upper respiratory symptoms, headaches, cold and flulike symptoms, and even cancer. Among the twelve common household molds, stachybotrys, known as black mold, produces mycotoxins that have been linked to severe health problems, even death.

In addition to mold, your home or office may also contain other contaminants, such as chemically scented candles, cleaners, air fresheners, fabric softeners, and products containing dyes or monosodium glutamate (MSG), which may produce detrimental consequences for your health and well-being.

Are you suffering from any of the following symptoms that could possibly be chemically triggered or mold-related illnesses or infections?

- Chest and nasal congestion

- Coughing, sneezing, wheezing
- Watery, dry, or sore eyes
- Skin irritations
- Headaches or migraines
- Asthma
- Fibromyalgia
- Weight gain
- Depression
- COPD (Chronic Obstructive Pulmonary Disorder)
- Pulmonary fibrosis
- Neurotoxicity
- Digestive and heart conditions
- Cancer

If you suspect mold in your home, office, or car . . .

1. Get tested! Seek certified mold testers and remediators.
2. Eliminate contaminants and chemicals immediately.
3. Seek doctors who practice holistic or functional medicine.
4. Walk away from any environment that interferes with your health.
5. Be an investigative sleuth and do everything you can to get and stay healthy!

Chapter 43
Chemical Sensitivity

Healthy citizens are the greatest asset
any country can have.
– Winston Churchill

After being exposed to toxic mold poisoning, I became sensitive to chemicals and synthetically made products. With four types of mold infiltrating my bloodstream, I developed pre-emphysema. I was weak and had trouble breathing. Microscopic fungal particles clogged my lungs. I went from being a bouncy fortysomething to bedridden. With alternative remedies, like oxygen therapy, infrared sauna, and vitamin IV, and by eliminating chemicals in my home and diet, I started regaining energy, had less brain fog, and slept better. My body was detoxifying, which was good but also challenging. Strong chemical scents made me physically ill. For months, I couldn't go into a mall, a grocery store, or even my son's school. When his parent-teacher conference was scheduled, I had to meet with his teachers outside the school's front door.

While multiple chemical sensitivity is a controversial topic among physicians, I can tell you that it's as real as real gets. Chemically scented candles give me migraines. That "new car" smell is actually the off-gassing of formaldehyde and other toxic chemicals used to treat materials for the carpet, dashboard, and seat covers.

Use paint with no volatile organic compounds (VOCs), which can give you headaches and flulike symptoms. If you've recently moved into a new home or office and developed allergies that won't go away, you might be chemically sensitive or, worse, have some level of toxic mold contamination in your building. (See previous chapter, "Mold.")

Instead of burning toxic scented candles, diffuse essential oils. They can clear your stuffy nose, prevent colds, enhance your mood, and help you sleep. I use them for cleaning, too!

Chapter 44
Sleep

*I love sleep. My life has the tendency to fall apart
when I'm awake, you know?*
– Ernest Hemingway

Who doesn't love to sleep? Not just lying in bed—I'm talking about the good stuff, when you wake up in the morning with a smile, your body is rested, and you're ready to rock the day—and let's just add this, the wrinkles are gone and your hair looks perfect.

Too much? Not necessarily. Getting enough sleep is an important part of being healthy inside and out. Restful slumber makes you look and feel better. It boosts your metabolism and immune function, aids digestion, and helps your memory. Adequate sleep can be your body's best defense against colds and aging, the race against the clock. But what if you don't sleep well?

One of the worst symptoms from my toxic mold exposure was that I couldn't sleep. There was no relaxation to be had. The sandman never visited. Rather, it felt like I had been plugged into an electrical socket and was being mildly electrocuted. I didn't just have restless leg syndrome; my whole body vibrated. Now how do you sleep like that? You can't. For a year, I felt like a walking zombie. It's no wonder that sleep deprivation is used as a form of torture.

Sleep allows your body to heal and repair itself from the stress and physical activities of the day. During sleep, hormones are released, and your immune system gets restored. If you're not getting good *Zs*, you're setting yourself up for the potential of having heart, lung, and kidney disease, stroke, cancer, and weight gain.

When you can't sleep well, you know there's nothing more important. You're a wreck the next day. You can't think straight, and you're moody. You want to eat everything in sight or nothing at all. Your reaction time is off, and you're exhausted. Sound familiar? And if your kids don't sleep well, you really need to consider making some modifications in your household. Lack of rapid eye movement (REM) sleep in school-aged children can affect essential growth hormones and cause headache, flulike symptoms, depression, acne, endocrine disruption, and even cancer. Got your attention yet?

Here are a few tips to help you find slumber-land more quickly and stay there longer:

1. Shut down electronics at least an hour prior to sleep. Yes, that includes cell phones and computers! Do you really need to send those texts or check how many "likes" you have on your latest social media post? No.
2. Stop caffeinated drinks at least eight hours before bedtime.
3. Use organic bedding, mattresses, and pillows.
4. Eliminate chemically scented laundry soap, fabric softener, and dryer sheets. Please.
5. Put electrical devices like alarm clocks several feet away from your bed or move them to another room.

Chapter 45
Clutter

Out of clutter, find simplicity.
– Albert Einstein

hate clutter. But I hate cleaning junk drawers even more. No one wants to do it, but from time to time, we all need to do a little spring cleaning. And you know what they say: One man's trash is another man's treasure. We all have things that may be valuable that we just don't use anymore. Selling those items on Craigslist, Amazon, or a resale shop could be a way to turn something that's been in a drawer or closet for months or (gasp!) even years into money.

Marie Kondo, bestselling author of *The Life-Changing Magic of Tidying Up,* asks her clients to pick up each item of clothing and ask if it brings them joy. If not, perhaps it will bring joy to someone else. Try it! It works!

Here's a tip to help you declutter fast. Start by spending four minutes cleaning a junk drawer or closet. (Yes, it might just lead to ten minutes or twenty!) Label four garbage bags:

- Donate
- Sell
- Throw away
- Save

If an item isn't useful and doesn't bring you joy, get rid of it!

Chapter 46
Wardrobe

A girl should be two things: Classy and fabulous
– Coco Chanel

have at least ten different styles. I have clothes for workouts, travel, professional engagements, date nights, and parent-teacher conferences. And then there's my favorite: Saturday night pizza-and-a-movie look. Fashion can change our mood and define who we are or, better yet, how we want to be perceived.

What is the look you're going for? If you haven't worn something, put it to use this week! Shop your closet. Mix things up. Ladies, step out of your comfort zone. Pair a floral top with striped pants. Look at popular fashion sites on the internet for ideas. Add some dazzling earrings or a pearl necklace to a simple T-shirt. Sarah Jessica Parker's character in *Sex and the City* wore a pearl necklace with her pajamas when she went to visit a friend late one night. That's fun, fierce and fabulous!

Guys, if you're into fashion, God bless you. I've noticed that more men are wearing bracelets, necklaces, and even tennis shoes with suits. This is awesome! There aren't as many options for you as there are for women. Check out your favorite men's magazines, websites, and social media for how to add a little allure and excitement to what you wear.

Chapter 47

Plan

A goal without a plan is just a wish.
– Antoine de Saint-Exupéry

D o you feel you're always rushing to get everything done and yet you never do? Although you know when holidays or birthdays are coming up, do you still end up scrambling at the last minute to buy gifts? Though I know darn well when I have to go on a trip, days or weeks in advance, often I find myself hurrying at the last minute to do the laundry, pay the bills, clean the house, and pack. Usually, I overpack and still forget something. Sound familiar?

One reason I wrote this book is to learn these lessons myself. So try this with me, won't you? Spend four minutes today looking at some projects that need to get done in the near future and plan them now. Buy birthday presents online and schedule their delivery on or before the birthday. Buy cards and store them for when you'll need them.

Consider these few tips to help you save time:
- Put an entire outfit, including jewelry or ties, on a hanger.
- Plan a week of meals.
- Buy gifts online months in advance.
- Pack early. Pretend your departure date for a trip is a few days earlier than it is.

Chapter 48
Live the Life You've Imagined

*Dream and give yourself permission to envision
a You that you choose to be.*
– Joy Page

What does your dream life look like? Where do you live? What are you wearing? Where are you going? What is your job? What are you doing in your free time? What or who inspires you? How do you want to feel? What course of action do you need to take to live the life you've always imagined?

We can say we want to be millionaires, or even billionaires, but if we fail to react to opportunities, take chances, or move forward, we may still be hoping and praying to win the lottery someday.

I intentionally put this chapter in the "Body" section of the book because you cannot live your best life unless you have a healthy body. Think about a time when you had a severe cold, the flu, or something worse that left you incapacitated. When I first went to be treated for toxic mold exposure, I barely had enough energy to sit up in bed and take a drink of water. That's not how I envision my best life to be.

So, with everything you've learned so far in this book about having a healthy mind and body, it's time for you to make a commitment. How can you live the life you've imagined?

Chapter 49
Being in Love

By the way, I'm wearing the smile you gave me.
– Unknown

Sweaty palms, shortness of breath, stomach pain, insomnia, inability to focus, nervousness, and feeling scared or worried about the future can be symptoms experienced when you're falling in love. The contrasting sensations of bliss, happiness, fulfillment, elation, confidence, joy, and divine intervention are also present. Being in love can make you feel a little crazy and terrifyingly amazing. You might take more risks and doubt yourself. Or, you might feel like a teenager, energized and unstoppable. Being in love can make you feel like your life is worth living.

Neurotransmitters like dopamine, oxytocin, and serotonin are released when the body experiences pleasure. Even something as simple as looking into the eyes of a loved one or getting a text message or phone call from that special someone can alter your overall sense of wellbeing, relieve stress, and fight depression. Thinking of a past or present romantic relationships can bring a smile to your face during difficult times. Recalling a kiss that sent a jolt of electricity through your body can dramatically enhance your mood. It can be the thing that makes your heart sing.

Chapter 50
Celebrate!

The more you praise and celebrate your life,
the more there is in life to celebrate.

– Oprah Winfrey

You've done the work; now celebrate because there's a new sheriff in town, a whole new *you!* Sometimes, we're our own worst critics. When someone pays us a compliment, we should accept it.

Stop criticizing yourself and start appreciating that you're here, reading this book, participating in this journey we call life. Honor your intentions and your new peace of mind. Be grateful for your health and happiness. Show gratitude in everything you do. Live life to the fullest each day, and don't look back. Choose to be happy or choose to be sad. It's your choice.

Create the life you've always dreamed you could live, starting now! We've all had hurdles. We've stumbled and fallen. We've been hurt physically and emotionally. We may have been on top of the world at one time but have descended into a darker, deeper, more contemplative space. Our souls want us to listen to the symphony of spectacular sights, sounds, and feelings our journey on Earth can offer. I know you can do this!

A shift in consciousness is happening now. Can you feel it? We're awakening to the possibility that there is more—more happiness, more wealth, more understanding for humanity. Perhaps it's simply wishful thinking on my part that I can be of service to others while creating more health and happiness in my life, but I'm going to take that chance. I'm a dreamer and a doer. Life is hard. At times, it's terribly messy. It doesn't turn out exactly how we planned, but if we open our hearts and minds to the possibilities that await us, we can transform our lives into more authentic and magical journeys.

Part IV

———

Healthy Body Journal

Write down a realistic goal here, such as, "I want to feel stronger and happier this month," and describe how you plan to achieve it.

_____

_____

_____

_____

_____

_____

_____

Oftentimes, we are too critical of ourselves. Take a moment to write something positive about your body.

_____

_____

_____

_____

_____

_____

_____

Repeat this exercise throughout your day: B.R.E.A.T.H.E. Take four minutes to relax your entire body and just breathe. How do you feel after breathing negativity or pain away? Record your thoughts and feelings about this exercise here.

_____

_____

_____

_____

_____

_____

Spend four minutes deciding how you can eliminate stress in your life.

_____

_____

_____

_____

_____

_____

_____

Do you notice that your mind becomes too busy, you get stressed, and you tend to overthink? What are the situations and who are the people that keep your mind occupied and racing at all hours of the day and night?

_____

_____

_____

_____

_____

_____

_____

In your calendar, write the times and days you can work out this week. Which exercises are your favorites, or which would you like to try?

_____

_____

_____

_____

_____

_____

List three options you can act on to enhance your current exercise program. If you're not exercising, why not?

_____

_____

_____

_____

_____

_____

_____

How many push-ups and sit-ups can you do in four minutes? _____

Keep a journal and count the number you can do after thirty days to compare.

How many squats can you do in four minutes? _____

One month later, how many squats can you do in four minutes? _____

Set your stopwatch for four minutes and do as many burpees as you can.

How did you feel after your four minutes?

_____

_____

_____

_____

_____

_____

_____

Try them again in thirty days and record your thoughts about this exercise. Can you do more?

_____

_____

_____

_____

_____

_____

_____

How many kicks can you do in four minutes? _____

What did you do for your playtime today? How did you feel after just four minutes?

_____

_____

_____

_____

_____

_____

_____

Name the five healthiest and unhealthiest foods you like.

_____

_____

_____

_____

_____

_____

_____

How can you include more vegetables, especially greens, in your diet?

_____
_____
_____
_____
_____
_____

Which healthy snacks can you swap with junk food?

_____
_____
_____
_____
_____
_____

Take a few raisins and spend one minute chewing each one. How did you feel as you ate the raisins? Anxious? In a hurry? Did you eventually relax?

_____
_____
_____
_____
_____

What allergic symptoms do you or your family members have?

_____
_____
_____
_____
_____

Spend four minutes shopping your closet to put together an ensemble that rocks! How do you feel when you are wearing something spectacular? Happy? Confident?

_____

_____

_____

_____

_____

Write down a few things you can do in advance to save time later.

_____

_____

_____

_____

_____

Perhaps you've always been a risk-taker and now you want to be more secure. It doesn't matter. Knowing what you know right now, knowing that you are wise enough to comprehend exactly what you want in your life's journey, spend four minutes writing down exactly how you *want* to feel.

_____

_____

_____

_____

_____

_____

_____

_____

_____

What prevents you from getting a good night's sleep? Are you anxious about something?

_____

_____

_____

_____

_____

_____

How will you celebrate your new, happier, healthier life?

_____

_____

_____

_____

_____

_____

Resources

What I Eat:

It's important to listen to our bodies. Most of the time, I don't eat breakfast. I drink it. I feel more energized when I can exercise the first thing in the morning on an empty stomach. In the morning I go straight to the coffee pot and start the process: making coffee, then blending it with one tablespoon each of cacao butter, collagen protein, and coconut oil. This combination fuels my body, my brain, and curbs hunger. If I am hungry in the morning, I'll make a small protein shake with greens, or have a hard-boiled egg.

Mid-morning, I juice carrots, beets, apple or pineapple, ginger, celery, and kale. For lunch I usually have a small salad with organic lettuce, spinach, kale, avocado, cucumbers, and a tiny portion of protein, like nuts or fish. I don't eat much chicken, pork or red meat, but I don't deny myself if I have a craving. Dairy products and sugar give me horrible stomach aches and make me bloated so I stay away from them. Having a piece of pizza can cause severe pain for a week! I always have raw nuts and raisins in the car. To stay hydrated, I drink water with lemon throughout the day.

Dinner is usually salmon, avocado, and steamed veggies with a drizzle of olive oil, salt, pepper and fresh herbs, and a glass of wine. Every day I have something sweet, preferably a homemade vegan chocolate chip cookie (or two). At bedtime I sip on chamomile tea with honey.

Enneagram Information:

- Take the Enneagram test to determine your type at www. wepss.com
- Ian Cron has an enlightening and entertaining podcast about the Enneagram called Typology. His books are brilliant resources for more Enneagram information. Check out his website at: www.ianmorgancron.com

Exercise Recommendations:

Here is a list of my favorite exercise programs. Search for a class near you at the following websites. Keep in mind, there are many different instructors and each one has a unique teaching style.

www.zumba.com

www.beachbody.com

www.cyclebar.com

www.butiyoga.com

www.crunch.com

Vitamins and Supplements:

I've tried a lot of vitamins over the years and only Isagenix has made a significant difference in my health and energy.

Here are some important website links:

www.shemanenugent.isagenix.com

www.shemanenugent.rocks

Functional Medicine:

Some of the all-natural healing remedies I used were infrared sauna, vitamin IV, hocatt, acupuncture, chiropractic, and oxygen therapy. Search for a doctor who practices functional medicine near you.

www.environmentalhealthcenter.com
www.hocatt.com

About the Author

Shemane Nugent has been a fitness instructor since 1980 and has appeared on MTV, VH1, Discovery, Entertainment Tonight, C-Span, FOX News, CMT, Outdoor Channel, MSNBC, and many other national and international radio and TV shows. After discovering her *MTV Cribs* home was contaminated with toxic mold and nearly killed her, Shemane dedicated her life to healing herself and her family through alternative remedies. She is on a mission from God to educate and inspire others, eat chocolate every day, and play with her dogs as much as possible.

For more healthy living information:

www.ShemaneNugent.Rocks